MARRIAGE BY THE BOOK

Book 6

Improving
Your Teamwork

Biblical advice for
Individuals
Couples
Small groups
Sunday school classes

Doug Britton, MFT
Marriage and Family Counselor

LifeTree Books
Sacramento, California
www.LifeTreeBooks.com

ISBN 1-930153-06-6

Except when otherwise noted, all Scriptures are taken from
the HOLY BIBLE, NEW INTERNATIONAL VERSION.
Copyright 1973, 1978, 1984 International Bible Society.
Used by permission of Zondervan Bible Publishers.

P200520050120

Printed in the United States of America

LifeTree Books
Sacramento, California

I want to express my deep appreciation to my sons Zach and Josh, their wives Holly and Paige, and countless friends for their many invaluable suggestions.

I especially thank my brother Gordon for his tireless editing and proofreading. Most of all, I am deeply grateful to my wife Skeeter for her many hundreds of insightful comments, painstaking editing, prayers and love.

•

Now to him who is able to do immeasurably more than all we ask or imagine, according to his power that is at work within us, to him be glory in the church and in Christ Jesus throughout all generations, for ever and ever! Amen (Ephesians 3:20-21).

BOOKS BY DOUG BRITTON

Conquering Depression: A Journey Out of Darkness into God's Light
Defeating Temptation: Biblical Secrets to Self-Control
Getting Started: Taking New Steps in My Walk with Jesus.
Healing Life's Hurts: God's Solutions When Others Wound You
Overcoming Jealousy and Insecurity: Biblical Steps to Living without Fear
Self-Concept: Understanding Who You are in Christ
Strengthening Your Marriage: 12 Exercises for Married Couples
Successful Christian Parenting: Nurturing with Insight and Disciplining in Love
Victory Over Grumpiness, Irritation and Anger

Marriage by the Book (eight-book series)
1: Laying a Solid Foundation
2: Making Christ the Cornerstone
3: Encouraging Your Spouse
4: Extending Grace to Your Mate
5: Talking with Respect and Love
6: Improving Your Teamwork
7: Putting Money in its Place
8: Fanning the Flames of Romance
Marriage by the Book Group Leaders' Guide

To see a current list of books by Doug Britton,
visit www.DougBrittonBooks.com.

Contents

Preface

Skeeter, our three boys and I used to go backpacking in California's Sierra Nevada mountains every summer. For some reason, as we hiked out of the mountains every year, the same thing happened: The boys moved ahead at their faster pace and Skeeter and I fell into a discussion about what the Bible says about the roles of husband and wife.

We both had gone to college in the 1960s and were steeped in the idea that "leadership" was an old-fashioned notion that had no place in a modern home. Parents should raise their children democratically, never saying, "No." Husband and wife were to be equal partners with no differences in roles. "Headship" and "submission" were foreign terms.

Once we became Christians, we learned the Bible presents another picture, that God defines different roles for husband and wife. Yet over the years we saw few people take the time to really study what God's Word says about this sensitive subject. We heard some say, "It's easy. The husband makes the decisions and the wife does what he says." It didn't take much Bible study to realize this simplistic formula didn't capture God's big picture.

Others went the opposite direction, looking for ways to discount Scriptures that define the husband's and wife's roles. They, too, missed God's plan.

Year after year, as we talked while hiking out of the mountains, as we continued to study at home and in church, and as I counseled hundreds of couples, we slowly came to see more and more of God's big picture. It is a picture both simple and complex. It is one based on mutual love and respect, with depths of riches we are still exploring.

God designed marriage to be a partnership, with husband and wife experiencing an intimate unity. Although there are differences in roles, neither is "the boss" in the way so many dread. Rather, each seeks to please the other, while gladly acknowledging the leadership of God's Holy Spirit.

Whether you already have a grasp of basic biblical principles, don't know what God's Word says about this subject or are struggling to break free from misconceptions, the following pages will encourage and challenge you.

Since this book deals with teamwork, it can be life transforming when husband and wife study together. Yet if your mate doesn't want to study, don't be discouraged. You will learn insights about *your* role and steps to take that can make a big difference in your relationship.

May God bless you with understanding and insight as you read, and may your marriage grow more light-filled and tenderhearted as you apply his Word in your lives.

Doug Britton

Introduction

We live in an age of countless and ever-changing opinions and theories about marriage. When we seek guidance, it is hard to know whom to believe.

Yet there is a dependable source to which we can go, one proven trustworthy and constant throughout history—the Word of God.

All Scripture is God-breathed and is useful for teaching, rebuking, correcting and training in righteousness, so that the man of God may be thoroughly equipped for every good work (2 Timothy 3:16-17).

The Bible covers it all, including communication, forgiveness, decision-making, finances and making love. God invented marriage. He knows how to make it work.

Improving Your Teamwork takes ageless truths from the Bible and helps you apply them in your marriage. It is the sixth in an eight-book series called *Marriage by the Book.* Although it stands as a complete book by itself, I encourage you to also read the other seven books, since they build on one another, each presenting the Bible's teaching on a different aspect of marriage. The eight books are:

(1) Laying a Solid Foundation

(2) Making Christ the Cornerstone

(3) Encouraging Your Spouse

(4) Extending Grace to Your Mate

(5) Talking with Respect and Love

(6) Improving Your Teamwork

(7) Putting Money in its Place

(8) Fanning the Flames of Romance

Each book is for individuals, couples and classes.

The books are designed to be studied by an individual, a couple, a small group or a church class. They also can be assigned as homework by a pastor, counselor or mentor. Although written for married people, these books also are excellent resources for those considering marriage.

Each book has six chapters, making it convenient for a six-week small group study program. The *Group Leaders' Guide for Marriage by the Book* shows how to set up and lead classes.

Each person should have his or her own book.

Numerous personal application questions (with spaces for answers) are scattered throughout this book. If you are studying as a couple, it would be best for each person to have a book. That way, both husband and wife can write answers and comments.

Names have been changed.

As you read, you will see that I have drawn upon the experiences of people I have counseled. The stories are true, but names and identifying details have been changed to maintain confidentiality.

Who is "Skeeter"?

If you have read some of my other books, you may remember that I sometimes referred to my wife as "Susan." In this book, I call her "Skeeter." Don't worry. Skeeter is Susan's nickname. I still am married to the same lively, intelligent, God-fearing woman.

Getting the Most from this Book

In *Laying a Solid Foundation,* the first book in this series, I wrote several guidelines to help you get the greatest possible benefit from studying. The following are some key points.

Examine your relationship with God.

Jesus declared, *"You must be born again" (John 3:7)* and added, *"I am the way and the truth and the life. No one comes to the Father except through me" (John 14:6).*

God created you and he loves you. Listen to Christ's invitation: *"Come to me, all you who are weary and burdened, and I will give you rest" (Matthew 11:28).* If you have not yet done so, I invite you to surrender your life to Christ by saying the following as a prayer:

> *"Dear Lord, I confess that I am a sinner. Please forgive my sins and accept me as your child. I invite you to be my Savior and the Lord of my life. I surrender myself to you in the name of Jesus Christ."*

If you prayed with sincerity, Christ accepted you into his Kingdom and you are now a Christian. Welcome to the family of God!

I accepted Jesus Christ as my Savior and Lord today. Thank you, Jesus!

_____   _____

Signature   Date

Not only will God help your marriage, he will transform your life. You have an exciting life ahead of you. These four suggestions will help you get started in your Christian walk:

- Tell someone that you accepted Christ.

- Read the Bible daily, starting with the Gospel of John in the New Testament.

- Join a Bible-believing church.

- Pray regularly.

Take the plank out of your own eye.

Most of us focus on our spouse's faults. Yet Jesus said, *"First take the plank out of your own eye" (Matthew 7:5).* As you read, focus on changes *you* should make, not on those you wish your spouse would make.

Write an answer to each question.

This book is designed to be interactive, with numerous "Personal Application" questions throughout to help you apply the material to your life. Think about each question and write your answer. In addition, underline key points as you read. Write notes in the margins or in a notebook.

If you find it difficult to write answers, I encourage you to overcome your reluctance or embarrassment. The more you involve yourself by answering the questions, the more the information will become part of you and the more you will change.

Study even if your spouse does not.

I hope you and your mate will study and learn together, but your spouse may refuse. In fact, he or she may say, "I don't have any problems. You're the one who needs help. Study by yourself."

What could be more frustrating? After all, your mate *does* have problems. Everyone does. You know it, and God knows it. But your spouse doesn't seem to know it.

However, even if your mate refuses to study, work through this book yourself. Don't say, "I'll read it, but only if you will." Instead, learn how to be the best husband or wife possible. God can perform miracles in your personal life and your marriage as *you* change.

Do not be overwhelmed by the information.

You may become discouraged by the many suggestions in this book, thinking you cannot follow them all. Don't feel condemned and do not try to do everything at once. There is a lot of material.

At the end of each chapter, "Putting It All Together" provides a place to identify one or two things you want to work on most. That should be enough for starters. Come back to the chapter later for fine-tuning.

Be appreciative if your spouse makes an effort.

Do not feel insulted if your mate follows some of the suggestions in these books. For example, if he or she asks you out to dinner, don't say, "You're just asking because you're supposed to." Or if your spouse apologizes for something, resist the temptation to respond, "You don't really mean it. You're only saying that because you know you're supposed to apologize."

The point of these books is to help people change. Be appreciative when your spouse makes an effort.

Do not give up when there are setbacks.

There is a pattern I see over and over: A couple experiences great improvements, then old problems reappear and one of them says, "I guess we haven't changed. I give up."

When this happens, don't give up. All marriages suffer reverses and difficult moments from time to time. Expect them, learn from them and press on.

Invite Your Mate to Study with You

I encourage you and your spouse to study this book together. Talking about these lessons can be exciting, even life-changing. Yet such discussions can degenerate into accusations, name-calling, anger and hurt feelings. The following guidelines will help you avoid common problems and get the most out of your time together.

Invite (but don't pressure) your mate.

Let your spouse know you would enjoy studying together, but don't start a fight over it. If your mate says "no," don't get into an argument. Instead, study alone.

Set up a regular time to talk.

Do not simply say, "We need to talk about this book sometime." Make specific plans. Agree on a schedule. For example, you could study together:

- Fifteen minutes every night after dinner or

- 7:00 to 7:30 p.m. Monday and Friday nights or

- 9:00 to 10:00 a.m. every Saturday.

Decide if you want to read separately before talking.

Some couples like to read a chapter separately and then get together to discuss it. Others prefer to read together and talk about the material as they go. Still others do both, reading when apart and then together.

Start with prayer.

Invite God to play a central part in your discussion. Ask him to:

- Show each of you what you need to work on the most.

- Give you grace and discipline to change.

- Help you talk with love and respect.

Read a few paragraphs, and then discuss them.

A common pattern for those who study together is for one person to read a few paragraphs out loud, after which both discuss the material. The second person then reads, followed again by a brief discussion. This process is often repeated for 20 or 30 minutes.

Don't worry if you find a point that is especially relevant and spend the entire time focusing on it. The idea is to deal with real issues, not just turn pages.

When you review the "Personal Application" questions, each can read his or her written answers or just share verbally.

Get involved.

Do not simply say, "I agree with that." Go into detail. Explain why you think what you do.

Share *personal* insights when you talk.

Talk about how the material applies to you, personally. Instead of pointing out what you think your mate should learn, discuss changes *you* should make.

Don' t get mad at your mate's comments.

If you tell each other your answers to "Personal Application" questions, you may sometimes be hurt by things your spouse says. Ask God to help you avoid reacting in anger or self-pity. There may be things you can learn from your mate's answers. Ask the Lord to help you respond with wisdom, understanding and love.

Write your own answer to each question.

Do not ask your mate to write answers for both of you. Write your own answers.

Ask before reading what your spouse wrote.

Your spouse may write thoughts, fears or temptations he or she desires to keep private. Agree not to read each other's answers without permission. As I wrote before, each person should have his or her own book if possible. Otherwise, think about writing your answers in separate notebooks to maintain privacy.

 *Personal Application*

Talk with your spouse and then write the day(s) and time(s) you will discuss this book together.

Chapter 1

See Yourselves

as a Team

*Submit to one another out of reverence for Christ
(Ephesians 5:21).*

Let me invite you to think about a man and woman compet-
ing for the Olympic Gold Medal in ice-skating. Chances
are good that you have watched many such couples and have
been enthralled by the beauty of their performance, the seemingly effortless athleticism of both, the strength of the man as
he lifted his partner high above his head and the graceful
movements of the woman as he showcased her.

As you imagine these two skaters, think about God's in-
tentions for marriage, for in many ways he wants us to be like
them.

Neither skater shows off. Rather, each portrays the other
in the best possible light. They are a team. The way they work
together determines whether or not they win a medal. Each is
responsive to the other's movements, automatically adjusting
speed and technique.

If one stumbles, the other doesn't stop to give an angry
lecture. Instead, he or she keeps skating while helping the
fallen partner recover quickly and gracefully.

The man takes the lead, yet he is highly sensitive to his
partner's strengths and weaknesses. Neither he nor his partner
is the big shot, for both follow the coach's instructions, not
their own spur-of-the-moment ideas. Each has willingly

worked to be a better partner, devoting countless hours to study and practice. They have a shared goal and work together to achieve it.

This couple is a team, two people seeking to give birth to something both lovely and magnificent, something that inspires and brings joy to others. They have created a partnership that brings beauty into the world.

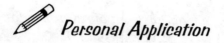 *Personal Application*

Describe an incident in which you and your mate functioned well as a team.

_____

Make Jesus Lord of Your Marriage

In Ephesians 5:22-24 and many other passages of Scripture, we are told that Christ is the head of the church and that we are to submit ourselves to him. This is similar to iceskaters submitting themselves to their coach, but even more so. Unless two people truly walk with the Lord and follow his commands, they cannot create the beautiful marriage he intends.

Consider one verse near the end of a passage about marriage: *"This is a profound mystery—but I am talking about Christ and the church" (Ephesians 5:32).* Here Paul explained that although he was writing about marriage, the deeper truth he was illustrating was the unity we are to have with God.

The most important thing you can do to improve the teamwork in your marriage is to follow God's leadership every day.

 Unless the LORD builds the house, its builders labor in vain. Unless the LORD watches over the city, the watchmen stand guard in vain (Psalm 127:1).

Glorify God in your marriage.

When you center your marriage in the Lord, not only will you experience a joyful relationship, you will also glorify God. When people look at you, they will see God's love in action. When people talk with you, they will hear you give him credit. Together you and your spouse can touch the world for Christ.

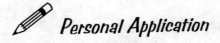 *Personal Application*

What is God's role in your marriage?

- ❏ We have not been aware of him.
- ❏ We know he is in charge, but do not follow his instructions.

❑ One of us tries to do things God's way, but the other one doesn't.

❑ We gladly follow his leadership.

What steps will you take to increase God's headship of your home?

Submit to One Another

Paul wrote, *"Submit to one another out of reverence for Christ" (Ephesians 5:21)*. James made the same point, saying that when we are wise we are submissive (James 3:17). These instructions are for *everyone*. Both husband and wife are to submit to one another.

Submissiveness is love in action.

When you read the word "submit," you may think of someone beaten in a fight surrendering to the victor. Or you may imagine a browbeaten man or woman giving in to an angry spouse.

That is not what the Bible means by "submit." In the Scriptures, submitting means serving. It means yielding our "rights" to serve the other person. It is what Paul wrote about when he instructed us to *"serve one another in love" (Galatians 5:13).*

Jesus, in spite of being the One who created the earth (John 1:3; Hebrews 1:2), took the form of a servant. When he did this, he gave us a perfect example of submission.

> *Do nothing out of selfish ambition or vain conceit, but in humility consider others better than yourselves. Each of you should look not only to your own interests, but also to the interests of others. Your attitude should be the same as that of Christ Jesus: Who, being in very nature God, did not consider equality with God something to be grasped, but made himself nothing, taking the very nature of a servant, being made in human likeness. And being found in appearance as a man, he humbled himself and became obedient to death—even death on a cross! (Philippians 2:3-8).*

The heart of Christianity is loving God and loving others (Matthew 22:36-40). Submission is demonstrating love in action, not being a doormat. As we strive to serve one another, we consider others as "better" or "more important" (New American Standard Bible) than ourselves (Philippians 2:3) and look out for their welfare. When I am submissive, I am concerned for what is best for my wife Skeeter, not what is best for me.

> *Nobody should seek his own good, but the good of others (1 Corinthians 10:24).*

 *Personal Application*

Pray for God to show you how submissive you are to your spouse, then score yourself.

0	1	2	3	4	5	6	7	8	9	10

Unsubmissive   Very submissive

List five ways that you have served your spouse in the past two weeks.

1.

2.

3.

4.

5.

Write a prayer asking God to help you develop a submissive attitude toward your husband or wife.

You are a Team

The ice-skaters have a goal: to skate as one. Each develops his or her own individual talents, and then they meld their abilities to create something of beauty.

Jesus, talking about the oneness he shared with God, prayed that all Christians *"may be one as we are one" (John 17:11)*. This remarkable prayer takes on special meaning for husband and wife since they are "one flesh."

 But at the beginning of creation God "made them male and female." "For this reason a man will leave his father and mother and be united to his wife, and the two will become one flesh." So they are no longer two, but one (Mark 10:6-8).

Some people think the Bible portrays marriage as a boss-employee or general-private relationship, but that is not the picture God paints. You can see this in the breathtaking description of marriage found in the Song of Songs. In this book about the marriage of the Shulamite woman and the king, each tries to outdo the other in love, growing in a relationship that celebrates their love and harmony. I encourage you to read the entire book.

Every morning, pray to remember the oneness you share with your spouse. Ask God to remind you of this special closeness throughout the day and to help you avoid drifting into living like roommates.

Personal Application

Read John 17:20-26 to see the oneness you and your spouse can have with each other and with God. How does this picture compare to what you normally experience?

Talk to God: *"Lord, I want to catch your vision of marriage. Please help me, every day, experience the wonderful, intimate sense of unity you intend between my spouse and myself. May I always remember that we are one. Also help me, I pray, to walk in unity with you. In Jesus' name."*

You Have Different Roles

Most biblical principles about daily living apply exactly the same to men and women. Both husband and wife are called to have a servant's heart, demonstrate respect, listen attentively and speak lovingly. That is why I waited until the sixth book in this series to address differences in roles. By first learning how the vast majority of Scriptures apply equally to men and women, you are less likely to form unbalanced views about headship and submission.

However, as you will see in several biblical passages quoted in Chapters 2 and 3, God assigns different roles to husband and wife. This is similar to the two ice-skaters. Although each submits to the other, one has the leadership role. In marriage, the man is assigned this role.

 Now I want you to realize that the head of every man is Christ, and the head of the woman is man, and the head of Christ is God (1 Corinthians 11:3).

The husband as leader

Let's look at the ice-skaters for a picture of biblical leadership in action. The male takes the lead as the couple skates, yet his leadership is directed toward accomplishing a mutual goal. As they glide over the ice, he seeks to showcase the woman. He does not seek his own selfish interests or consider himself the star of the show.

He is not lazy. He prepares himself for the contest, for if he does not know how to skate well or is out of practice, he will hurt the team.

In practice sessions, he discusses the program with his partner and they design their routine together. He comfortably acknowledges areas in which she has more talent or expertise.

The wife as follower

The woman skater willingly follows her partner's lead, secure in the knowledge that they are a team and that she plays an equally important role. In practice sessions, she feels free to analyze their moves and discuss the program with him. Yet when they perform, she throws herself into skating, gladly following his lead without questioning his every move.

The wife as co-ruler

Some think the Bible teaches that women are weak, fragile creatures. That is far from the truth. In Chapter 3, you will read about many strong women in the Bible who disprove this stereotype.

Here's a way to get the right picture: Imagine you are in a deserted building. A gang of armed thugs has trapped you and is about to attack. Things look bad—there's no way you can handle them all. "Help!" you scream.

Suddenly a timid serving girl appears at your side and fearfully asks, "Can I get you a cup of water, sir?"

In desperation you yell, "Not that kind of help! I need a warrior!"

God created Eve to be Adams's "helper" (Genesis 2:18). Some think this means the wife's job is to be a domestic servant or attendant to her husband, always ready to get a soft drink or run to the store for something he wants.

God had a different kind of helper in mind. The Hebrew word translated as "helper" in Genesis 2:18 is used 22 times in the Old Testament. It always refers to someone of power who aids a person facing a serious problem. In fact, in 15 of the 22 times it refers to God as the one who helps. For example:

We wait in hope for the LORD; he is our help and our shield (Psalm 33:20).

I lift up my eyes to the hills—where does my help come from? My help comes from the LORD, the Maker of heaven and earth (Psalm 121:1-2).

God, speaking of both Adam and Eve, said, *"Let them rule" (Genesis 1:26).* Eve was created as Adam's helper to rule with him.

Let's return to the example of the skaters and examine the attitude of the woman. Does she feel less important than her partner because he has the lead role? Not at all. She is excited as they pursue their goal together. She is secure in her position as an equal member of the team.

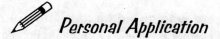

Personal Application

What does the Bible mean by "helper"?

The Big Picture

Have you ever driven into a new city and become confused as you tried to follow instructions to a friend's house? It's easy to do. When I first drive into a new area, I like to study a map of the whole city before looking for a specific address. That way, I have an idea of the big picture and am less likely to get lost.

My purpose in this chapter is to illustrate God's big picture of partnership in marriage before looking at the details.

To better see this, let's look at five key themes that will show up many times in the following pages. Each, as you will see by the time you finish this book, comes from the Word of God. Any one point taken separately only shows part of the picture. You need all of them to form the big picture.

1) Husband and wife should experience unity.

A married couple is "one." God wants husband and wife to experience the unity he has decreed. This unity reaches its fullest potential when the couple is united in Christ, acknowledging him as Lord.

2) Husband and wife are to submit to one another.

Each submits to the other, considering the other's welfare as more important than his or her own. When decisions are made, they are usually made as a team. Neither dominates.

3) The roles of husband and wife are similar.

In one sense, there is little difference in roles. God expects both husband and wife to practice all the virtues discussed in the first five books in this series: self-confrontation, commitment, forgiveness, prayer, love, servanthood, encouragement, forbearance, understanding, respect and courteous speech. These biblical principles, and many more, apply equally to husband and wife.

4) The husband is to be a servant-leader.

The husband is the leader in the partnership, but not in the sense some think. He is not a big shot. Rather, he serves his wife. He is responsible to love her, provide oversight of the home and submit to Christ's leadership.

5) The wife is to honor her husband as leader.

The wife willingly acknowledges her husband's leadership, secure in the knowledge that this is God's will. She does not feel like a second-class citizen, for she realizes that submission is not degrading. She knows she is equally loved and valued by God and uses her gifts and abilities to the fullest.

The following passage beautifully illustrates some of these points. When you read the terms "submit" and "head," avoid thinking of a boss-employee relationship. Instead, think of the ice-skaters or of Solomon and his wife as described in the Song of Songs. That's the biblical picture.

Submit to one another out of reverence for Christ.

Wives, submit to your husbands as to the Lord. For the husband is the head of the wife as Christ is the head of the church, his body, of which he is the Savior. Now as the church submits to Christ, so also wives should submit to their husbands in everything.

Husbands, love your wives, just as Christ loved the church and gave himself up for her to make her holy, cleansing her by the washing with water through the word, and to present her to himself as a radiant church, without stain or wrinkle or any other blemish, but holy and blameless. In this same way, husbands ought to love their wives as their own bodies. He who loves his wife loves himself. After all, no one ever hated his own body, but he feeds and cares for it, just as Christ does the church—for we are members of his body. "For this reason a man will leave his father and mother and be united to his wife, and the two will become one flesh." This is a profound mystery—but I am talking about Christ and the church. However, each one of you also must love his wife as he loves himself, and the wife must respect her husband (Ephesians 5:21-33).

Personal Application

Why is it important to understand all five of the above points?

_____

Evaluate Yourself

Let me invite you to evaluate how well you do in several areas of teamwork. The husband's self-evaluation starts on this page. The wife's will follow in a few pages.

Husband's Self-Evaluation

Many men do not have a good grasp of what God means by leadership. Common mistakes made by husbands are described in the next few pages. If a lot of them describe you, don't be discouraged. You will read about solutions in the following chapters.

As you read, ask yourself if you:

- Try to control your wife.

- Are self-centered.

- Are distant or uninvolved.

- Abandon your leadership role.

Signs that you are controlling

You are probably too controlling if the following comments describe your attitudes or actions. Check each statement that applies to you.

☐ I am the boss. It is my job to run the family and it's my wife's job to do what I say.

☐ I often give my wife instructions.

☐ I decide how we will spend money.

☐ I quote Scriptures about submission to my wife.

☐ I expect my wife to ask permission before going anywhere, although I simply announce I'm leaving.

☐ I think my wife's opinions are naïve or stupid.

☐ I am impatient when my wife is not submissive.

☐ I think most of our marriage problems would be solved if my wife were more submissive.

☐ I withhold affection if I don't get my way.

 *Personal Application*

Describe any ways in which you think you are controlling or domineering.

Ask your wife what she thinks and write her answer here.

_____

Signs that you are self-centered

You are probably too self-centered if the following comments describe your attitudes or actions. Check each statement that applies to you.

❑ My wife's main role in life should be to help me.

❑ My wife should put most of her time and attention into supporting me in my career.

❑ My wife should join me in all my ministry activities.

❑ When I am thirsty, it's my wife's duty to get me a glass of water.

❑ My wife should take care of tasks I give her to make my life easier.

❑ My wife should only prepare meals I like.

❑ My wife should keep the house spotlessly clean.

❑ My wife shouldn't bother me with problems.

❑ I don't like the idea of "giving my life for her."

❑ I might be willing to give my life for my wife, but wash the dishes? Never!

❑ I don't know how to serve my wife.

❑ I don't understand my wife.

❑ My wife is too needy.

❑ I want things done my way.

✎ *Personal Application*

How self-centered are you?

What changes should you make to be less self-centered?

_____

Signs that you are distant

Some men spend little time with their wife or children. You are probably removed or uninvolved if the following comments describe your attitudes or actions. Check each statement that applies to you.

❑ I come home after work, eat dinner and then watch TV without talking much with my wife.

❑ I do not communicate a lot with my wife. I don't really know what she thinks or does during the day.

❑ Sometimes it seems as if we live in two different worlds.

❑ I bring lots of work home from my job.

❑ My major responsibility is to bring home a paycheck. Raising our children is my wife's job.

❑ I rarely compliment or praise my wife.

❑ I spend more recreation time with my friends than with my wife.

❑ I earn a good living, don't run around with other women and don't get drunk. What more could any woman want? She doesn't know how good she has it.

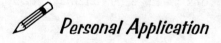 *Personal Application*

If someone watched you for a week, how involved would this person say you are in your wife's life?

What are steps you should take to become more involved?

_____

Signs that you abandon leadership

Some men, rather than being too bossy, are too passive when it comes to making decisions. You probably abdicate your leadership role if the following comments describe your attitudes or actions. Check each statement that applies to you.

❑ I pretty much let things happen.

❑ I know there are times when I should provide godly guidance, but I rarely do so.

❑ I see things we ought to talk about, but don't bring them up.

❑ When my wife brings up problems, I don't want to discuss them.

❏ I am uncomfortable making decisions.

❏ I don't want to be domineering, so I back off.

❏ My wife angers easily. I don't want to upset her.

❏ I expect my wife to discipline the children.

❏ I do not train our kids in spiritual matters.

❏ I am so passive that our kids control the family.

✎ *Personal Application*

Do you exercise leadership? Score yourself from 0 to 10.

0	1	2	3	4	5	6	7	8	9	10
Abandon leadership						Exercise leadership				

List any ways in which you have abandoned leadership.

Wife's Self-Evaluation

Many women have trouble accepting the principles of headship and submission and make one or more of the following mistakes. If any of them describe you, don't be discouraged. You will read about solutions in the following chapters.

As you read, ask yourself if you:

- Reject your husband's leadership.

- Try to take over.

- Do not support your husband's endeavors.

- Take the role of a doormat.

Signs that you reject his leadership

You probably have an unbiblical attitude toward headship and submission if the following comments describe your attitudes or actions. Check each statement that applies to you.

☐ Before marrying, I developed independence as a single woman. I don't want to give it up.

☐ I have a position of authority at work. It's hard to switch roles when home.

☐ I don't know what the Bible says about roles.

☐ I don't agree with what the Bible says about roles.

☐ I think the idea of "submission" is demeaning.

☐ I'm afraid my husband will take advantage of me, so I'm always on my guard.

❑ My husband is not a good leader, so I ignore what he says.

❑ I don't respect my husband, so I argue with him.

❑ "Submission" is old-fashioned.

Personal Application

Do you treat your husband as your leader? Score yourself from 0 to 10.

0	1	2	3	4	5	6	7	8	9	10
I don't										I do

If you did not score 10, what are ways in which you have not treated him as the leader?

Signs that you are controlling

Some women do more than just reject their husband's leadership. They try to take charge. You probably are too controlling if the following comments describe your attitudes or actions. Check each statement that applies to you.

❑ Not only do I reject my husband's headship, I try to take the leadership position.

❑ I have a domineering personality.

❑ I am persistent, knowing that eventually my husband will give in if I continue to make my point.

❑ I overwhelm my husband with the intensity of my feelings, letting him know how *important* things are to me.

❑ I frequently correct my husband.

❑ I get angry and give bitter speeches about how I wish my husband would act.

❑ I am manipulative and use subtle methods to get my way.

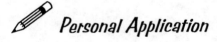 *Personal Application*

Describe any ways in which you think you are controlling or domineering.

Ask your husband what he thinks and write his answer here.

Signs that you are not supportive

Do you support your husband in his personal life, ministry and career? You are probably not as supportive as you should be if the following comments describe your attitudes or actions. Check each statement that applies to you.

❏ I am consumed by my career.

❏ I am so concerned about my own issues that I give little thought to supporting my husband in his personal life, ministry and career.

❏ I seldom encourage him in his endeavors.

❏ I rarely compliment or praise him.

❏ I bring up his failures a lot.

☐   I spend so much time and energy helping others, I don't have much left for my husband.

☐   I put a tremendous effort into being a great mother, leaving little time or energy for my husband.

✎ *Personal Application*

Describe what you do to support your husband.

What are some steps you could take to be more supportive?

Signs that you have become a doormat

Some women take the idea of submission to an unhealthy extreme. You probably have an unhealthy viewpoint about submission if the following comments describe your attitudes or actions. Check each statement that applies to you.

☐ My constant focus is on pleasing my husband.

☐ I tiptoe around, fearful of his anger or displeasure.

☐ I feel like a "doormat," always there for him to wipe off his dirty shoes.

☐ I do not develop my own talents or gifts.

☐ I avoid discussing anything that he might disagree with.

☐ I don't know much about our financial situation.

☐ I often let my husband do the thinking, as if I did not have any brains.

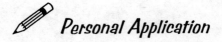 *Personal Application*

Do you feel like a doormat in your marriage?
☐ Yes ☐ No

Why did you answer as you did?

Putting It All Together

Key point: Think of yourself and your mate as two ice-skaters trying to perfect your teamwork. Serve your spouse.

•

Memory verse: *"Submit to one another out of reverence for Christ"* *(Ephesians 5:21).*

 *Action Plan*

Choose one or two things from this chapter to work on this week.

1.

2.

Chapter 2
Husbands, Practice Servant-Leadership

*The Son of Man did not come to be served,
but to serve (Matthew 20:28).*

Few concepts in the Bible have been so misunderstood, misused or disliked as the principle of the husband's headship. Domineering men misuse it. Feminists reject it. Many sincere Christians struggle with it. Yet there is no question about it: The Bible says the man is the head of his wife.

Now I want you to realize that the head of every man is Christ, and the head of the woman is man, and the head of Christ is God (1 Corinthians 11:3).

For the husband is the head of the wife as Christ is the head of the church, his body, of which he is the Savior (Ephesians 5:23).

What does God mean by saying the husband is the head? He is obviously talking about leadership. Yet as you study the Bible, you will see it is a different type of leadership than what many think.

See Yourself as a Servant

Jesus' disciples thought being a leader simply meant having authority. They assumed it meant being in charge, ordering others around. The Lord surprised them when he told them they had it all wrong. Being a leader, he said, meant being a servant.

Jesus called them together and said, "You know that the rulers of the Gentiles lord it over them, and their high officials exercise authority over them. Not so with you. Instead, whoever wants to become great among you must be your servant, and whoever wants to be first must be your slave—just as the Son of Man did not come to be served, but to serve, and to give his life as a ransom for many" (Matthew 20:25-28).

Christ illustrated how a leader should act by washing his disciples' feet, a task normally assigned to a servant (John 13:1-10). After washing their feet, he said:

Now that I, your Lord and Teacher, have washed your feet, you also should wash one another's feet. I have set you an example that you should do as I have done for you. I tell you the truth, no servant is greater than his master, nor is a messenger greater than the one who sent him. Now that you know these things, you will be blessed if you do them (John 13:14-17).

Have you thought being the leader means you are better or more important than your wife—or that you are the big shot? If so, pray for a new attitude and walk in humility for, *"Pride goes before destruction, a haughty spirit before a fall" (Proverbs 16:18).*

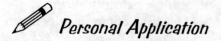

Personal Application

How would your wife describe you?

- ❑ Big shot
- ❑ Mean one moment, nice another
- ❑ Servant-leader
- ❑ Other _____

Describe two things you did to serve your wife in the past week:

1.

2.

What attitudes must you change to be the type of servant-leader God desires?

Write a prayer asking God to help you make these changes.

Do not be controlling or domineering.

But, you might say, the Bible says a church overseer or elder *"must manage his own family well" (1 Timothy 3:4-5).* It says he must "manage." Doesn't that mean he's the boss?

Bruce, a man I knew decades ago, took this idea to the extreme. He was studying to be a minister at the time and said he was exasperated because his wife would not obey him. His solution? To "spank" her with a switch. To him, there was no difference between wife and child. Both were to obey him and disobedience was to be met with physical chastisement.

I was appalled when I heard him say this and tried to convince him he was wrong, but was unsuccessful. He soon moved away, and I never learned the conclusion to this sad story.

Yes, the Bible says a leader must "manage" his family, but it also says he must manage "well." The husband is the leader, *but the way he manages is what counts.*

The "I'm the boss" style of leadership is not scriptural and does not work well. Marriage is not an owner-slave, sergeant-private or parent-child relationship.

If you order, lecture or complain a lot, you are likely to wind up with an unhappy wife, one who is angry, bitter or fearful. That makes sense, doesn't it? Would it be smart to be stern, domineering, lecturing, disrespectful and insensitive, then expect your wife to be sweet, loving and submissive? Of course not. Yet that is exactly how some men act.

If you desire a close relationship, follow the example of Jesus. Give yourself, sacrifice yourself, for your wife. Be a servant-leader. As you read the following pages, *focus on your responsibility to love and serve, not on your authority to make decisions.*

✎ *Personal Application*

Ask your wife if you seem controlling. Don't be angry or defensive if she says, "Yes." Tell her you appreciate the feedback and would like some examples. Write them here.

Look for ways to serve, not be served.

If you watch people at a picnic, you may see a couple seated at a table, talking with friends, when the husband decides he'd like a glass of water. Instead of getting it himself, he asks his wife to get it for him. She (probably) does so.

What's wrong with this picture? Maybe nothing, but then again, maybe a lot. The question is, does he also serve her, or does he see himself as a king who should be waited upon?

Although the Bible refers to a man's wife as his "helper" (Genesis 2:18), it does not mean she is a serving girl. Each person is to be servant to the other, so each should be glad to get the other a glass of water. As Jesus said, *"It is more blessed to give than to receive" (Acts 20:35).*

Instead of asking, "Could you get me a glass of water?" say, "Honey, I'm getting a glass of water. Would you like one?" It's a wonderful thing to serve. It is something entirely different to expect to be served. As Paul wrote, *"Each of you should look not only to your own interests, but also to the interests of others" (Philippians 2:4).* He also wrote:

 In this same way, husbands ought to love their wives as their own bodies. He who loves his wife loves himself. After all, no one ever hated his own body, but he feeds and cares for it, just as Christ does the church (Ephesians 5:28-29).

If you face a decision, or if you feel grumpy, ask yourself, "How can I best love and serve my wife at this time?" Instead of focusing on what you would like, think about what would be best for her and for you as a couple. Although it's okay to also consider your desires, in most of your actions and decisions primarily take into account:

- Her convenience, not yours

- Her desires, not yours

- Her reputation, not yours

- Her comfort, not yours

- Her emotions, not yours

The Bible says a husband is to be willing to sacrifice his life for his wife just as Christ gave his for the church (Ephesians 5:25). Since you must be prepared to die for her, you should be much more willing to sacrifice for her in life. Do not sit around expecting her to sacrifice for you. Instead, give yourself for her.

✐ *Personal Application*

Do you expect to be served? ❏ Yes ❏ No

Should you make more offers and fewer requests?
❏ Yes ❏ No

If so, what changes will you make?

Write a prayer asking God to soften your heart and help you prioritize your wife's welfare.

Feel free to make requests periodically.

Now that I've emphasized serving your wife, let me add a few words of balance. It's not always wrong to ask your wife to do something. If she is moving toward the kitchen, it's perfectly fine to ask, "Could you bring me a glass of water when you come back?" If you are sick, you should feel free to ask for some aspirin.

Or if you've just collapsed into a chair after hours of strenuous work and your wife is nearby, it may be appropriate to say, "Honey, would you mind getting me a glass of water? I'm exhausted." Then again, she may be just as exhausted as you and would appreciate it if you offered to get her a glass of water.

There are other exceptions. For example, people working together naturally make requests of one another. If you and your wife are working on a project, it might be reasonable to ask, "Could you please give me the scissors?"

Along similar lines, if your wife says, "Darling, I'd love to serve you. Please allow me to do that," the most gracious response would be to say, "Thank you." Allow your mate to express her love. Just be sure that in your day-to-day life, she also experiences you serving her.

Help your wife develop her talents and gifts.

God has given your spouse talents and gifts. Help her recognize and develop them. Do not be threatened if she is more creative, intelligent or talented than you in some areas. Instead, rejoice in her gifts. Her abilities can strengthen your marriage.

The scriptural view of women is one of strength. Read about the virtuous woman (Proverbs 31:10-31), Deborah, a prophetess who judged Israel (Judges 4) and the daughters who helped rebuild Jerusalem's walls (Nehemiah 3:12). These all were women with demonstrated abilities and strength.

Does your wife hold back from developing her gifts because of lack of confidence? Is she overly dependent on you or insecure in her own abilities? If so, your task is clear: Encourage and support her.

The following are ways to help your wife develop her abilities and strength:

- Point out the things she does well. Help her identify her gifts. Encourage her in them.

- Praise her a lot. Rarely criticize.

- Watch the kids one night a week so she can attend a women's Bible study, take a college class or develop a hobby. Do not try to isolate her because you are afraid she'll meet someone else and leave you. Be the type of husband God expects you to be to ensure your marriage's safety.

- Ask her for advice and prayer about problems and decisions you face personally and as a couple.

- Acknowledge her abilities and expertise. If she is better with numbers and details, suggest she do the family finances.

- Be sure she is actively involved in financial decisions and planning.

- Agree on projects in which she is the leader and you are the follower.

 *Personal Application*

List five of your wife's strengths.

1.

2.

3.

4.

5.

Encourage her by telling her you recognize these strengths. Check this box after you do so.

❏ I told my wife that I see these strengths.

Ask her if there is one talent that you can help her develop.

The talent I will encourage:

Steps I will take to encourage her:

Express Love

Countless women live heartbroken lives, certain their husbands don't love or cherish them. In many cases, this is not because the husband actually says, "I don't love you." Rather, it is because he doesn't say, "I love you."

If your wife thinks you do not love her, do something about it. Don't just say, "That's dumb. She should know I love her."

Paul's chief command to husbands was to *"love your wives, just as Christ loved the church" (Ephesians 5:25).* He followed this up by describing the intensity with which Christ loved the church.

 Husbands, love your wives, just as Christ loved the church and gave himself up for her to make her holy, cleansing her by the washing with water through the word, and to present her to himself as a radiant church, without stain or wrinkle or any other blemish, but holy and blameless. In this same way, husbands ought to love their wives as their own bodies. He who loves his wife loves himself. After all, no one ever hated his own body, but he feeds and cares for it, just as Christ does the church—for we are members of his body (Ephesians 5:25-30).

According to the Bible, even a king can't be sure of protecting his throne by brute force alone. *"Love and faithfulness keep a king safe; through love his throne is made secure" (Proverbs 20:28).* Since a king, with all his power, should secure his throne by love, you also should secure your marriage by showing your wife you love her.

Not only will you secure your marriage, but you will also make it easier for her to be a godly wife. It is much easier for her to submit to someone who loves her than to someone who doesn't seem to care.

Here are ways to show your wife you love her:

Cherish her.

Make your wife feel special, that you are delighted to be married to her. Do not live as roommates. Instead, treat her as a wonderful gift from God. The Bible says, *"He who finds a wife finds what is good and receives favor from the Lord"* *(Proverbs 18:22).*

Make her your closest friend.

Jesus quoted from Genesis when he said, *"The two will become one flesh"* *(Matthew 19:5).* The idea of "one flesh" refers to your sexual union, but it encompasses much more than that. It means you are to make your relationship with your spouse your primary relationship, putting her above parents, brothers, sisters, children, friends or coworkers. Do not put more time or energy into any other relationship.

Demonstrate love through words and actions.

Show your wife you love her. Don't say, "Of course I love her. She knows that." Instead, look for ways to express love every day. Say these special words: "I love you."

Ask yourself the following questions to evaluate how well you express love. Rate yourself from 0 to 10 on each one.

- "0" means, "I don't do this at all."
- "10" means, "I do this to my wife's satisfaction."

My score (0-10)

I express love every day through my words .... _____
I express love every day through my actions .... _____
I spend one-on-one time with her daily. .... _____
I invite her to go on a date weekly. .... _____
I often write notes or phone to say, "I love you".... _____
I invite her to go on holidays, just the two of us. ... _____

I often give her little gifts or flowers. .... ____

I frequently hug or touch her non-sexually............. ____

I let her know that she is special to me. .... ____

Regardless of how spiritual you appear on the outside, how much money you make or how nice your house is, *if you do not demonstrate love, you are being exceedingly cruel.* Your wife needs to experience your love. You are not a godly leader, or even an adequate leader, unless you show her that you love her.

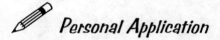 *Personal Application*

If someone were to ask your wife if she feels loved, what would she say?

What are two specific ways you will express love to her this week?

1.

2.

After you do these two things, write her responses.

Her response to #1:

Her response to #2:

Respect Her

Some people say that women need love and men need respect. That's true, but the flip side is also true. Women need respect and men need love.

Show good manners, but don't stop there.

I remember Fred, a man who thought showing respect meant opening the door for his wife and holding the chair for her when she sat down to eat. Although she appreciated these gestures, she was frustrated because he never seemed to listen to her opinions.

Showing respect is much more than being polite. It means noticing and valuing her creativity, compassion, intelligence, organization and other gifts. It means treating her as an adult, not a child—as a partner, not an underling.

Value her opinions, thoughts, attitudes, feelings, knowledge and abilities.

Learn from your wife.

Some think that since the husband is the leader, God only speaks to the man. That's not true. God spoke through his angel to a married woman and told her she would conceive and have a son—Samson. He told her, not her husband Manoah, how to raise Samson (Judges 13:1-7).

Later, she and Manoah talked together with the angel. Afterwards, when Manoah realized the man they had spoken with was an angel, he was terrified and said, *"We are doomed to die! ... We have seen God!" (Judges 13:22).* His wife responded with words of logic and comfort.

In 2 Kings, we read about another married woman. She, not her husband, recognized Elisha as a holy man of God and suggested that they prepare a room for him to stay in when he was in town (2 Kings 4:8-10). God rewarded them with a son for their efforts.

Since your wife is your helper, listen to her wisdom and insights. She knows you in ways that no one else does. Respect her as a gift from God. Ask her advice and learn from her.

 *Personal Application*

What are some things your wife said recently that you disagreed with or didn't understand?

Now pray, asking God to help you see through her eyes. Do not rush through your prayer. Write any new insights here.

How will you use these new insights?

Study 1 Peter 3:7.

Peter packed a lot of instructions to husbands in the following verse. As you read, evaluate your attitudes toward your wife and identify adjustments you need to make. Then meditate on this verse when you go through tense times.

Husbands, in the same way be considerate as you live with your wives, and treat them with respect as the weaker partner and as heirs with you of the gracious gift of life, so that nothing will hinder your prayers (1 Peter 3:7).

- **You are to be considerate.**

   "Be considerate as you live with your wives" is translated differently in the King James Bible (KJB) and the New American Standard Bible (NASB). The KJB says to live with her "according to knowledge" and the NASB says to be "understanding."

   Each translation highlights a slightly different aspect of the same theme: Know, or understand, your wife. Seek to see through her eyes. Become aware of how she thinks and feels. Be sensitive to her feelings and life circumstances. Look for ways you can minister to her.

- **She is your partner.**

   She is your partner, your counselor and your helper. Do not look down on her or belittle her. If you have trouble respecting your wife, read the section titled "But he hasn't earned my respect" in Chapter 3. The points in this section, written for a wife who doesn't respect her husband, also show how God wants you to look at your wife.

- **She is the weaker partner.**

   Christians disagree about what Peter meant when he wrote that the woman is weaker. Some think this refers to PMS mood swings, while others suggest it means the wife is physically weaker. Some think it refers to a wife's gentleness, delicacy or emotional makeup. Still others suggest it refers to Eve being the first to be deceived by sin (Genesis 3:1-6). Another interpretation is that men might be considered stronger, or more aggressive, because of the male hormone testosterone.

Our understanding of this has been influenced, no doubt, by our culture. Although we do not know for certain what Peter meant, remembering this verse can help you be considerate and supportive with your wife.

For example, if your wife experiences PMS or goes through menopause, you should be sympathetic and patient. Many women who go through hormonal changes feel like they are on drugs and find it extremely difficult to control their emotions.

- **She is heir with you of the gracious gift of life.**

    You are heirs, together, and share a wonderful inheritance. Both of you, if each is a believer, will spend eternity with Christ.

- **Your prayers are hindered if you treat her poorly.**

    You cannot have a close walk with God when you disrespect your wife. John made a similar point when he wrote, *"If anyone says, 'I love God,' yet hates his brother, he is a liar"* (1 John 4:20).

Praise her.

Follow the example of the husband in Proverbs 31 who praised his wife, saying, *"Many women do noble things, but you surpass them all"* (Proverbs 31:29). Let your mate know you respect her intellect, sensitivity, good cooking and organizational abilities. Also praise her physical appearance.

If you have children, honor your wife as a mother.

In God's sight, it is both special and important to be a mother. In our culture, however, many undervalue motherhood. If your wife is a mother, honor and support her. Follow the example of Adam, who honored his wife by naming her Eve, or "Life-giver."

Adam named his wife Eve, because she would become the mother of all the living (Genesis 3:20).

Tell your wife you appreciate all the effort she puts into being a mother. Praise her to your children, pointing out her many virtues. Always speak respectfully when talking with her or about her.

 *Personal Application*

Do you need to show your wife more respect?
❑ Yes   ❑ No

If so, list three ways in which you will be more respectful.

1.

2.

3.

_____

Get Involved

Jonathan seemed puzzled. His wife Wendy had insisted they come for counseling and he couldn't figure out why. As far as he could see, everything was okay in their marriage, yet she seemed to think they were in a crisis. He explained his point of view: "Sure, I work long hours. And when I come home I need to relax, so I watch TV. Things haven't worked out for us to go out much, but we did go to a movie a few months ago. We don't get into screaming matches and don't have any big problems. I'm just like every other guy."

Mike had a similar story about his marriage with Joyce: "Look, I don't eat dinner with the family but who would with all the arguing? I'd rather eat alone and watch TV. I'm not a bad guy. I love my wife and I put up with her, but I can't stand to talk with her; she's always complaining. Besides, she never wants to make love."

Wendy and Joyce felt abandoned and unloved. They had dreams of emotionally intimate marriages, yet their husbands seemed satisfied with casual relationships. Each woman was resentful that the only type of intimacy her husband seemed to want was sex.

Countless women have similar frustrations and are desperately unhappy, although their husbands think their marriages are doing great. Many have given up their dreams, resigning themselves to living like roommates.

God made you the *leader* in your home. Do not be passive, saying, "I just want peace and quiet," or, "I just want to do what comes naturally." Get busy. Make your relationship with your wife a priority. Help out with the kids. Eat dinner with the family. Take walks together. Go on dates. Talk with her. Learn what she is thinking and feeling. Tell her about your life experiences, dreams and fears.

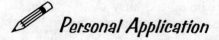 *Personal Application*

What are ways in which you should be more communicative and involved with your wife?

Take the Initiative

Joe and Margie were a typical couple seeking to improve their marriage. They had run into seemingly insurmountable problems and came to me for counseling. At the end of the first session, I gave them an assignment to read the first book in this series of books and do the exercises. When they saw me the following week, Margie had done the work, but Joe explained he had been "too busy." This pattern continued, with Joe either being too busy or forgetting the homework each week. Margie became increasingly discouraged.

Joe did not understand his wife's feelings until I explained to him that, to her, not doing the homework "proved" he did not love her. She thought if he really cared, he would have thrown himself into his assignments. Each time he failed, it seemed as if he was saying, "Our relationship isn't worth my effort." To his credit, once Joe understood his wife's feelings, he made an about-face and went to work on his homework.

Wives everywhere, not just those in counseling, voice similar frustrations. Many desperately wish their husbands would take the initiative to suggest marriage-building activities such as praying together every morning, studying the Bible, reading marriage books, talking after work or going to home fellowship groups.

If this describes your wife, every day you do not take the initiative may be a day of disappointment or heartbreak. It is not neutral to do nothing.

Notice that I am emphasizing taking the initiative. It is not enough simply to go along with your wife's proposals. It's good to say "yes" when she makes suggestions, but you too should bring up ideas. Show leadership: Surprise her tomorrow by suggesting a Bible study, praying together or doing something else to enrich your relationship.

Personal Application

Do you need to take more initiative to suggest marriage-building activities? ☐ Yes ☐ No

If so, write your plan for at least one thing you will suggest within two days.

Lead by Example

Your example is much more important than anything you say. Although the following instructions were not written specifically for husbands, they show five key ways in which you can be an example.

 Set an example for the believers in speech, in life, in love, in faith and in purity (1 Timothy 4:12).

You may find it easier to act Christ-like while at work than when at home. This is normal. At work, the relationships are not nearly as intense, and you usually know that in a few hours you will leave for the day. Your Christianity is put to the real test when you are home.

 *Personal Application*

When you are with your wife, what kind of an example do you provide in each of the areas Paul identified in 1 Timothy 4:12?

- "0" means, "I really need to work at this."
- "10" means, "I do great at this."

Speech. *My score (0-10)* _____

Life. *My score (0-10)* _____

Love. *My score (0-10)* _____

Faith. *My score (0-10)* _____

Purity. *My score (0-10)* _____

Choose two areas that need improvement and write your plans to change.

First area:

My plans:

Second area:

My plans:

Lead in Righteousness

Your most important duty as a husband is to center your life in the Lord and lead your family in ways that honor him. Be like Joshua, who said, *"But as for me and my household, we will serve the LORD" (Joshua 24:15).*

Blessed are all who fear the LORD, who walk in his ways. You will eat the fruit of your labor; blessings and prosperity will be yours. Your wife will be like a fruitful vine within your house; your sons will be like olive shoots around your table. Thus is the man blessed who fears the LORD (Psalm 128:1-4).

Be a man of prayer.

Most of us must discipline ourselves to pray as much as we should. Yet when you think about it, prayer is an indescribable privilege. When you pray, you communicate with God, the One who made everything. Through prayer you can become more Christ-like and grow in your ability to lead your household.

> *Devote yourselves to prayer, being watchful and thankful (Colossians 4:2).*

Read the Bible daily and live by it.
We *need* to read the Bible. Not only do we learn God's instructions, we also are changed spiritually. God dwells in his Word.

> *For the word of God is living and active. Sharper than any double-edged sword, it penetrates even to dividing soul and spirit, joints and marrow; it judges the thoughts and attitudes of the heart (Hebrews 4:12).*

There is another reason to become familiar with the Bible. In 1 Corinthians 14:35, women are instructed to ask their husband questions at home. Study the Word so you can answer questions with knowledge instead of simply stating your own opinions.

Seek ways to grow together as Christians.
Do not be a one-day-a-week Christian. Talk with your wife about your experiences with God every day. Share insights from your personal Bible study. Ask if she learned anything interesting from her Bible study. Talk about ways the Lord helped you on the job or opportunities you had to tell others about him.

There are countless other ways to lead your family in righteousness. Invite your wife to pray with you every day. Study the Bible or a devotional book together. Ask other Christian couples over for dinner.

As you seek to be a godly leader, do not pressure your wife to join you in Christian activities. Instead, invite her. If you are too forceful, you may push her away.

Do not lead your wife in ungodly behavior.

Larry, a man I counseled, wished his wife Connie was more uninhibited when they made love, so he took her to a strip joint for inspiration. Other men I have talked with have asked their wife to watch pornographic movies for the same reason. The eventual result for Larry, as for most men who do such things, was that his wife became more and more disgusted with their sex life. She increasingly saw sex as dirty and uninviting, instead of a holy and beautiful way to express and receive love.

Do not lead your wife in ungodliness. Learn a lesson from Ananias, a man who led his wife in lying to God. God killed them both (Acts 5:1-11).

Follow your leaders.

God instructed us to obey our leaders and submit to their authority (Hebrews 13:17) unless their instructions violate the Bible. They can motivate us to stay on God's path.

Over the years, I have noticed that men who take a hard, unbalanced line when it comes to the wife's submission often give themselves much leeway when it comes to submitting to church authorities.

Such a man, while demanding submission, is often unsubmissive himself. He excuses his attitude on the basis of conscience or theology, yet doesn't grant his wife the same freedom to disagree with him. He needs to loosen his grip on his wife and, at the same time, reevaluate his attitude toward his church leaders.

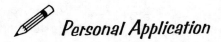

Personal Application

How well do you lead in prayer, Bible study and other aspects of righteousness?

0	1	2	3	4	5	6	7	8	9	10

Poorly   Actively

What is one area in which you wish to improve?

Write your plan.

Provide Oversight and Direction

Some people think that since the husband is called to be a servant-leader, he should be passive—like a traditional servant, waiting to receive instructions. Some go so far as to think that since he is a servant, the wife is the leader!

This, of course, flies in the face of the verses we have examined about the husband's leadership. Look at Jesus' example. Although he said he came to serve, not be served

(Matthew 20:25-28), he also taught his disciples and made decisions that affected them.

Being a servant-leader does not mean you are not a leader. Although God wants you to lead by example and place your wife's welfare above yours, he also expects you to provide oversight and direction.

Stay aware of what's going on.

Leadership is more than simply reacting to problems. You cannot be a good leader unless you are aware of what is going on in each family member's life. How aware are you? Score yourself from 0 to 10 on each of the following.

- "0" means, "I don't know what's going on."
- "10" means, "I am *very* aware."

My score (0-10)

I know how my wife is doing spiritually .... _____

I know how my children are doing spiritually .... _____

I know how we are doing financially .... _____

I am aware of my wife's problems or concerns............ _____

I know how the kids are doing with homework .... _____

I am aware of how my wife is doing at her job .... _____

I am aware of my wife's hopes for the future .... _____

I know about any needed house repairs .... _____

The following is a short list of things that should be happening in every family. Check each box that is true in your marriage.

- ☐ We have family Bible studies.

- ☐ Our finances are under control.

- ☐ Family members get along well.

- ☐ My wife feels supported by me.

☐ The kids go to bed on time.

☐ The kids and I do our share of housework.

☐ Our car and home maintenance is up-to-date.

☐ My wife is happy about how I talk with her.

☐ We have talked with our children about sex.

☐ We fellowship with other Christian couples.

☐ We go to bed early enough to get enough sleep.

☐ We go to church regularly.

 *Personal Application*

Have you provided godly oversight in your family? Ask the Lord if there are areas that need attention. If there are, write one topic here.

Now ask your wife how she thinks you do at providing oversight and direction. Also ask her if there are areas in which she thinks you should be more involved. Write her answers here.

Pray when you see a problem.

When you see something that you think needs attention, the most important thing you can do is pray. In fact, it may be all that God wants you to do. If you intervene, you may get in the way of the Holy Spirit's work.

- **Pray for God's direct help.**

    Ask the Lord to help with the situation or circumstances.

- **Pray for wisdom.**

    Your first impressions might not be accurate. The steps you think are needed might not be what the Lord wants. Ask God for wisdom.

- **Pray for a loving and respectful attitude.**
  Ask the Lord to help you identify and deal with your own shortcomings before considering changes your spouse should make (Matthew 7:1-5). Also ask him to help you get rid of any anger or bitterness and to love your wife.

- **Pray about whether or not to talk with your wife.**
  There may be times when God expects you, as the leader of the family, to share your observations with your wife. For example, if you see her drifting away from God, neglecting her gifts or developing a problem with alcohol, it may be right and loving to speak with her.
  However, don't be a critical person, bringing up everything on your mind. Pray about the following three questions before talking:

  - **Should I say anything?**
    Perhaps God only expects you to pray about the problem and then leave it in his hands.

  - **When should I speak?**
    Timing is critical. If your wife is cooking dinner or talking on the phone, it probably is not the best time to start a sensitive conversation.

  - **How should I speak?**
    Speak in love and gentleness, even if you need to confront a serious problem. Be sure she knows you are speaking out of concern for her welfare. Study Galatians 6:1.

Bring problems up as a friend.

If you bring up an issue, speak with love and respect. As Paul wrote, *"Husbands, love your wives and do not be harsh with them" (Colossians 3:19).*

Why did Paul say *"and do not be harsh with them"?* The obvious answer is that many husbands tend to be harsh. Think about Colossians 3:19 the next time you are tempted to speak harshly.

 As charcoal to embers and as wood to fire, so is a quarrelsome man for kindling strife (Proverbs 26:21).

When you talk, speak gently and keep it short. Once you share your observations, leave your wife in God's hands. Don't keep repeating yourself, even if she disagrees with what you said.

Invite your wife to join you in making a change.

If you identify a problem that appears to require action, remember that your wife is your partner. *Make plans as a team.* Imagine, for example, that you would like to start praying together more often. Instead of announcing a prayer schedule, discuss your desire and ask if she would like to help make a plan.

If you discover your expenses are greater than your income (regardless of who is doing the excess spending), present the problem and together set up a time to talk. When you meet, respectfully summarize the situation as you see it and ask your wife what she thinks. Then create a budget together.

Make a decision on your own when needed.

There may be times when you try to make decisions as a team, but you are unable to come to an agreement and can't put off making a decision. On these occasions you need to make a final decision, since you are the leader.

Your decision may be to do what you think is best, but it also could be to do what your wife thinks is best. The point is, you are the leader and are responsible to make a decision when necessary.

Some husbands, in an effort not to be domineering, back away from making any decisions. Yet making decisions is part of what leadership is all about. On several occasions Jesus, although he was a servant-leader (Matthew 20:28), made decisions contrary to what his followers wanted (Matthew 16:22-23; Mark 5:18-19; Luke 9:54). On each occasion, it was because he knew what was for the best, not because of selfishness.

On rare occasions you may need to be firm. Mark found himself in such a position when his wife Lucy ran up huge debts on their charge cards. Even after talking, she was seemingly unable to cut back her shopping, so he closed most of the accounts and took her name off the remaining ones.

A word of caution: If you think you have been too passive, don't overreact and become a dictator. Wait until you finish this book before deciding if you need to change your leadership style.

Personal Application

Which, if any, of the above guidelines about providing oversight and direction have you neglected to follow?

What changes will you make?

Putting It All Together

Key point: Practice servant-leadership. Show your wife that you cherish her.

•

Memory verse: *"The Son of Man did not come to be served, but to serve" (Matthew 20:28).*

 *Action Plan*

Choose one or two things from this chapter to work on this week.

1.

2.

Chapter 3
Wives, Honor Your Spouse's Leadership

*Wives, submit to your husbands, as is fitting
in the Lord (Colossians 3:18).*

Skeeter's note: Since this chapter is written specifically for women, I asked Doug if I could add my own comments. He said, "That's a great idea." Look for "Skeeter's notes" in boxes like this.

As we have already seen, *all* Christians are called to be submissive to one another (Ephesians 5:21; James 3:17). Submissiveness is the mark of a Christian. It is love in action. It is being concerned for others' welfare more than your own.

God does not want either partner in a marriage to be domineering or controlling. However, in addition to mutual submission, God has assigned husband and wife different roles. Think again of the ice-skaters in Chapter 1. The husband is called to be a servant-leader and the wife to be what Skeeter likes to call a "fearless follower."

Many people have trouble understanding or accepting these roles, thinking they make women less important than men. This uneasiness is felt by many Christians as well as non-Christians. When the subject of submission comes up in church, it is often greeted with nervous laughter or anger.

Why does this happen? One reason is that headship and submission teachings are sometimes used to justify the "Honey, go get me a beer" mentality. Another is that some think the follower is less valuable than the leader, that the leader has all the brains and the follower isn't supposed to think. Additional reasons abound, many of which are understandable. For example, it's not unusual for a wife to think:

✓ "My father was a dictator and my mother went along with it. I don't want to be like her."

✓ "I'm afraid my husband will treat me like his father treated his mother."

✓ "I was abused in a previous relationship."

✓ "My husband is abusive."

✓ "I have an absentee husband."

To add to these understandable concerns (all of which are addressed in this chapter or in Chapter 6), there is the hostility of the secular culture around us. Many scorn the idea of male leadership, thinking it barbaric and abusive. In fact, many people look down on the idea of serving anybody unless it is to make money.

God looks at things in an entirely different light. Even though Jesus created everything that exists (John 1:3), he came to serve, not be served (Matthew 20:28). He taught us about a servant's attitude when he said, *"For he who is least among you all—he is the greatest" (Luke 9:48).* He also said, *"Whoever wants to be first must be your slave" (Matthew 20:27).*

Jesus was not a wimp or a doormat. He showed us that serving, when done with the right attitude, is powerful and godly. When a woman acknowledges her husband's leadership she is not surrendering to a conqueror, nor is she saying she is worth less than her husband. Rather, she is reflecting the picture of the church as it submits to Christ (Ephesians 5:22-24). A woman who follows her husband's leadership does so because she loves Jesus; she submits because, in her heart, she is submitted to Christ.

Skeeter's note: I am often helped to submit graciously when I remember to first submit to God, then submit to Doug. Just submitting to Doug makes me nervous.

The following passages establish the husband's headship. As you read, ask the Holy Spirit to help you understand God's plan for a beautifully functioning team. You will see that God's picture of a wife is not a weak, beaten-down woman, but one who is strong, secure in the love of Christ and in her partnership with her husband. She embraces the fact that God has named her husband the servant-leader.

The head of the woman is man (1 Corinthians 11:3-12).

In the rest of this long passage, Paul also points out that man is born of woman. Each needs the other.

Wives, submit to your husbands as to the Lord. For the husband is the head of the wife as Christ is the head of the church, his body, of which he is the Savior. Now as the church submits to Christ, so also wives should submit to their husbands in everything (Ephesians 5:22-24).

The scope of submission is great (but, as you will see later, not absolute). Remember that in verse 21, Paul called for mutual submission.

Skeeter's note: In our marriage, we discuss almost everything, often arriving at a terrific third idea better than either of us could think of alone. Doug rarely makes decisions affecting both of us on his own.

But sometimes he does. One major decision Doug made that I disagreed with was to write this "Marriage by the Book" series. Now that I've seen Doug's books help people I know and love, I'm glad he stuck with his decision. I'm also glad I supported his decision even before I saw he was right.

Wives, submit to your husbands, as is fitting in the Lord (Colossians 3:18).

It is fitting in Christ for you to follow your husband's leadership.

Skeeter's note: A Christian friend recently said to me, "But the real word in the Greek doesn't mean 'submit,' does it?" It does. The Greek word translated "submit" is "Hupotasso." It is the same word used in passages that tell us to submit to Jesus.

Likewise, teach the older women to ... train the younger women to love their husbands and children, to be self-controlled and pure, to be busy at home, to be kind, and to be subject to their husbands, so that no one will malign the word of God (Titus 2:3-5).

Again, we read the wife is to be subject to, or follow, her husband's leadership.

Wives, in the same way be submissive to your husbands so that, if any of them do not believe the word, they may be won over without words by the behavior of their wives, when they see the purity and reverence of your lives. Your beauty should not come from outward adornment, such as braided hair and the wearing of gold jewelry and fine clothes. Instead, it should be that of your inner self, the unfading beauty of a gentle and quiet spirit, which is of great worth in God's sight. For this is the way the holy women of the past who put their hope in God used to make themselves beautiful. They were submissive to their own husbands, like Sarah, who obeyed Abraham and called him her master. You are her daughters if you do what is right and do not give way to fear (1 Peter 3:1-6).

Should a woman submit to a non-Christian husband? Yes. She can greatly influence her husband by demonstrating a gentle and quiet spirit.

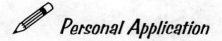 *Personal Application*

What has been your attitude about leadership and submission?

What changes, if any, do you think God would want you to make in your attitude in view of the above verses?

Give an example of a situation in which you followed your husband's leadership.

_____

Serve from Strength

When God created Adam and Eve, he created *both* in his image and said let *"them"* rule (Genesis 1:26-27). God created Eve to be co-ruler with Adam. Although your husband is the leader in your partnership, God wants you to be strong, wise and productive. *God does not say that you are less important, less capable or less loved than your husband.* Rather, he gives each of you different roles.

 There is neither Jew nor Greek, slave nor free, male nor female, for you are all one in Christ Jesus (Galatians 3:28).

Early in our marriage, Skeeter and I were exposed to an extreme teaching that said the husband should make all the decisions and "protect" his wife by handling all contact with the outside world. Prior to this, Skeeter had been a vivacious, energetic person. However, in a misguided effort to be submissive, she thought she should leave all the thinking to me.

As a result, she became more and more fearful of the outside world until she even felt intimidated talking on the telephone with a school secretary. After we realized the error of this doctrine, it took much study and effort for her to regain her confidence.

Although there may be times when looking to your husband for support or protection is appropriate, do not become a helpless, fearful person. Study each of the following verses and let these strong women be examples for you.

- Miriam was a prophetess. She led all the women as they praised God (Exodus 15:20-21).

- Deborah, a prophetess, judged Israel (Judges 4:4- 5:31).

- Jael killed Sisera, an enemy leader pursued by the Israelite army (Judges 4:17-22).

- Women ("daughters") helped rebuild the walls of Jerusalem (Nehemiah 3:12).

- Queen Esther risked her life to save the Jews (book of Esther).

- The virtuous woman was extremely capable and industrious, both at home and in commerce (Proverbs 31:10-31).

- Anna was a prophetess (Luke 2:36).

- Mary Magdalene, Joanna, Susanna and other women supported Jesus and the apostles out of their own means (Luke 8:1-3).

- Lydia was a businesswoman (Acts 16:14).

- Priscilla engaged in the trade of making tents with her husband. They also ministered together (Acts 18:2-3, 26).

These women were strong and active, not unthinking "doormats." You and your husband are a team. Do not say, "I'm a slave and you are my master." Instead, say, "I am the queen and you are the king." Your message to your husband should be, "In Christ, I am strong, wise and have great worth, and I gladly acknowledge your leadership."

Offer advice and participate in decision-making.
When you and your husband make a decision, give him the fullness of your counsel, delivered politely, as a friend. You are a partner and can strengthen your partnership with wisdom and insight.

Consider decisions as if everything depended on you. If you are making a budget, become aware of all the family's financial details. Get involved. Do not just respond to your husband's ideas.

Skeeter's note: How does the picture of a wise woman square with calling the woman the weaker "partner" (or "vessel" in the Greek) (1 Peter 3:7)? As Doug discussed in Chapter 2, there are many ideas about how women are weaker.

Peter's use of the word "vessel" makes me think he meant our physical bodies. I'm thinking here of our chemical makeup—our hormones—as well as our muscles.

Although modern women now compete in almost every arena, they still don't take on men in the Olympics. But when it comes to thinking and creativity, women do as well as men.

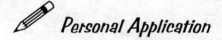 **Personal Application**

Describe the type of strong wife you would like to be.

Draw Close to God

It is not possible to live a Christ-like life without Christ's help. The same guidelines written for men in Chapter 2 also apply to you. Be a woman of prayer and of the Word, reading the Bible daily. Walk close to God and grow in the fruit of the Spirit (Galatians 5:22-23). Your relationship with God is more important than anything else.

Charm is deceptive, and beauty is fleeting; but a woman who fears the LORD is to be praised (Proverbs 31:30).

Drawing close to God gives you the power to be a godly woman. It also sets a wonderful example for your husband as he sees *"the purity and reverence of your life" (1 Peter 3:2).*

Skeeter's note: I have found Doug is no substitute for Jesus. There are some things only our Savior can supply.

God speaks to women as well as men.

Judith asked me about a verse that says, *"The head of every man is Christ, and the head of the woman is man, and the head of Christ is God" (1 Corinthians 11:3).* She wondered if this means Christ only speaks to the husband who then passes the message on to his wife.

The answer is, "No." We all have the privilege of prayer and can speak to God and hear from him. Anna was a prophetess who heard from God (Luke 2:36-38). When Jesus taught about prayer in the Sermon on the Mount, he spoke to crowds of people, women as well as men (Matthew 6:5-13). When God sent the angel Gabriel, he spoke directly to Mary (Luke 1:26-38) and only later to Joseph.

✎ *Personal Application*

Does your marriage sometimes suffer because you are
not walking in the Spirit? ❑ Yes ❑ No

If so, how?

Write one way in which you will draw closer to God.

What is your plan to accomplish this goal?

Choose to Submit

The Bible does not tell your husband to "subject" you. (He wouldn't be much of a servant-leader if he tried, would he?) Rather, God's Word instructs you to submit to his leadership, to acknowledge him as your head. This is a decision God wants *you* to make out of reverence for Christ.

Submission is not grudgingly giving in to your husband. Rather, it is acknowledging that God knows the best way to run a home. It is choosing to obey God.

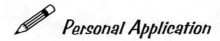 *Personal Application*

Write a personal commitment to look upon your husband as your leader.

_____

Have a submissive attitude.

Submissiveness starts in the heart. Although your actions are important, your attitudes are even more so. As Jesus said, *"Out of the overflow of the heart the mouth speaks" (Matthew 12:34).*

By adopting the right attitude, you help set the stage for a good marriage and make it much easier for your husband to comfortably do his job as servant-leader. Demonstrating a godly, submissive attitude is one of the most powerful things you can do to bless your husband, your marriage and your life.

 A wife of noble character is her husband's crown, but a disgraceful wife is like decay in his bones (Proverbs 12:4).

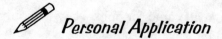 **Personal Application**

Do you need to change your attitude toward your husband? ☐ Yes ☐ No

Write a prayer asking God to help you make the specific changes that are needed in your attitude.

Do not be afraid he will take advantage of you.
Fear often keeps a woman from wholeheartedly submitting to her husband. Peter warned of this when he instructed women to be *"like Sarah"* and added, *"do not give way to fear" (1 Peter 3:6).*
One big fear you may have is that your husband will take advantage of you if you are submissive. You think he will boss you at whim and bully you.

In my counseling experience, the opposite usually happens: The husband becomes more attentive and concerned when his wife chooses to submit. Fearless submission is a particularly powerful tool for encouraging passive husbands to get involved.

Kelly and Walt came for help. They had only been married a few years, but their home had become a battlefield. Kelly found herself becoming increasingly verbally aggressive and sometimes even hitting Walt. She didn't trust him with the finances and thought if she didn't watch him like a hawk, he would secretly siphon away all their money and leave her. Walt had become distant and angry.

After a few meetings Kelly told me, "I feel I've been a contentious and angry wife and I want to change." To her credit, once she made that decision, she plowed into the Word of God to learn all she could.

In a short time, Kelly's demeanor changed completely and she interacted with Walt in a gentle, trusting way. Walt responded by easily forgiving her anger and working through other issues they faced. She was delighted to see he didn't take advantage of her and in fact became the servant-leader she had dreamed of.

Do all men respond like this? It has been my observation that most do. However, this isn't guaranteed. Some men take advantage of a wife's submissive attitude, demanding more and more and giving little in return. In Chapter 6, you will read about how to respond if this happens. For now, let me suggest that you put aside your fear and approach your husband as God wishes.

> *Skeeter's note: I'm not afraid that Doug will boss me around. But I'm careful not to lose who I am by submitting. This is because, as Doug wrote, I lost my sense of self by unbalanced submitting in the past.*
>
> *I guard against this by reminding myself that Doug is best served by the most intelligent, productive, interesting, creative, godly version of me. I must maintain and train my strengths to augment his own, and to make up for his weaknesses.*

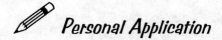 **Personal Application**

Have you been afraid your husband would take advantage of you if you were submissive?
❑ Yes ❑ No

Do you have other fears about submitting to your husband? If so, what are they?

Follow His Leadership

Have you ever been placed in a position of responsibility or authority, yet when you tried to exercise leadership, you encountered resistance or complaints? If so, you know how discouraging or humiliating that can feel.

The way you respond to your husband as leader has a dramatic impact upon how he fulfills his role and upon how well your marriage functions.

 The wise woman builds her house, but with her own hands the foolish one tears hers down (Proverbs 14:1).

Your husband may feel uncomfortable as a leader. This is not helped if you treat him disrespectfully or often tell him he does a poor job. Listen to yourself as you go through the day. Do you treat your husband as your leader? Or do you do some of the following? Check each box that describes you.

- ☐ I often tell him *what* to do.
- ☐ I frequently tell him *how* to do things.
- ☐ I step in and take over projects if he does not do them quickly enough.
- ☐ I take over if he doesn't do things the way I want.
- ☐ I am a back seat driver.
- ☐ I'm a complainer.
- ☐ I argue a lot.
- ☐ I secretly do things I know he disapproves of.
- ☐ I talk about his faults behind his back.

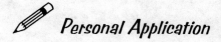 *Personal Application*

Do you treat your husband as your leader? Score yourself from 0-10.

0	1	2	3	4	5	6	7	8	9	10
I don't										I do

Write specific changes God is calling you to make in the
way you speak to him or respond to his leadership.

1.

2.

3.

Can you think of one thing your husband asked you to
do, something that did not violate your conscience, that
you have refused or ignored? ❑ Yes ❑ No

If so, what is it?

How do you think God wants you to respond?

You are not called to submit to all men.

Every Christian is supposed to submit to every other Christian (Ephesians 4:21). That is to say, we are to be unselfish and concerned for others. But when it comes to authority, a woman is uniquely submissive to her husband, not to other men.

Do not wait for your husband to be perfect.

As I counseled Greg and Ellie, it soon became obvious that Ellie constantly criticized Greg. She thought he didn't run his business right, chose the wrong parking places at the mall and was a lousy husband. I went to work with them, sharing observations and giving each one homework projects.

When I told Ellie she was violating God's Word by rejecting Greg's headship and constantly berating him, she protested, "But he doesn't have my best interests at heart."

Ellie had slipped into a common mistake, that of thinking she had to fight her husband to get him to do the right thing.

The results, predictably, were awful. The sad thing was that Greg really did want to be a good husband.

Your husband is flawed. Everyone is. God knew Adam was imperfect when he told Eve, *"He will rule over you" (Genesis 3:16).* Your husband will make mistakes. This is particularly true if you are married to an unbeliever. Yet even in this potentially difficult situation, the Bible instructs you to be submissive (1 Peter 3:1-6). Do not wait for your husband to "earn" the right to be your leader.

Marge talked with me years after she and Jack had come for marriage counseling. It was easy to remember them. Marge's domineering personality and Jack's remoteness were both extreme. Yet, she said, the Lord turned their marriage completely around.

As we talked, Marge said a turning point for her was when I pointed out that *of course* Jack was imperfect. Before then, she had nursed a condemning attitude. Once she accepted his humanness, she became more understanding and forgiving. She treated him more as a leader and criticized him less.

Although she felt free to occasionally voice frustrations, she now said them politely and lovingly. Jack appreciated her new approach and he changed too, becoming involved with his family.

Learn a lesson from Marge. Don't say, as some do, "I'll be submissive if you love me as Christ loved the church." Instead, do things God's way now. Be the best wife you can be.

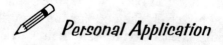

Personal Application

Have you held back from accepting your husband's leadership because of his faults? ❏ Yes ❏ No

Write a prayer, asking God to help you accept your husband's leadership in spite of his imperfection.

Do not quarrel.

Remember Ellie, the woman who pointed out her husband's faults throughout the day? Her explanation was, "I'm just being honest."

She thought being honest meant voicing every critical thought that came to her mind and questioning almost every decision he made. She was surprised to realize she had slipped into serious sin. She had become a quarrelsome wife. Once she understood her error, she cut back on her criticisms and backseat driving. The tension level in their marriage dropped dramatically.

Express your opinions and participate in decision-making, but learn when to stop. If you don't like something your husband does, do not wear him down until he gives in.

A quarrelsome wife is like a constant dripping (Proverbs 19:13).

Better to live on a corner of the roof than share a house with a quarrelsome wife (Proverbs 21:9).

Better to live in a desert than with a quarrelsome and ill-tempered wife (Proverbs 21:19).

A quarrelsome wife is like a constant dripping on a rainy day; restraining her is like restraining the wind or grasping oil with the hand (Proverbs 27:15-16).

Do these verses mean you can't ever bring up a problem or disagree? Of course not. Talking about real issues is crucial to a good marriage. But learn to recognize when you have stopped discussing and have started nagging, complaining and quarreling. Remember, *"A gentle and quiet spirit"* is of *"great worth in God's sight"* (1 Peter 3:3-4).

Skeeter's note: There are no verses about quarrelsome husbands, which flags quarrelsomeness as more of a problem for us women.

Deal with PMS and menopause.

For many wives, the most difficult time to be gentle and quiet is when they experience premenstrual syndrome (PMS) or go through menopause. Women I have counseled have shared the following practical tips:

- Seek medical help.

- Eat a proper diet and exercise.

- Identify early signs that you are beginning to experience PMS.

- Alert your husband when you see the warning signs. Ask for patience.

- Do not talk about serious or distressing subjects if they would push you over the emotional edge.

- If you start to lose control:

  ✓ Remind yourself you know what's going on.

  ✓ Call time-out. Stop talking.

  ✓ Pray.

  ✓ Ask for prayer.

Skeeter's note: When I can't lift something, I call for Doug and his muscle; when I become hormonally unglued, I call for Doug and his stable, unflappable hormone-free opinion.

 *Personal Application*

Check the appropriate box if you sometimes:

❑ Complain
❑ Quarrel
❑ Nag

What triggers your quarreling (hormones, your mother coming to visit, etc.)?

How well does quarreling work? Check the appropriate box that describes how your husband responds when you quarrel.

❑ He gets mad.
❑ He speaks reasonably.
❑ He withdraws.

If you are quarrelsome at times, write a plan to overcome this.

Do not be sneaky or manipulative.

Some people teach that women should trick their husbands into doing what they want. Ignore that advice. When you manipulate your husband, you step outside the boundaries of partnership and headship. It's more honest to make straightforward suggestions.

Does this mean it's wrong to wait until a romantic dinner to suggest a trip to Hawaii? Not necessarily. Choosing a good time to speak makes sense. The key is not to pressure your husband to say, "Yes."

Follow his decisions.

Most decisions should be made collectively, as a team. But if you can't agree, give him the message, "This is my opinion, but I will support you if you think you must make a decision now instead of waiting until we agree." Follow the Bible's instructions in 1 Peter 3:6, where we read that wives should be *"like Sarah, who obeyed Abraham and called him her master" ["lord" in the New American Standard Version]*.

Skeeter's note: I see Doug not as my boss or drill sergeant, but as my friend, my lover and my lord. This makes it much easier to submit to him.

Some women are bothered that I call Doug "lord," even though that's what Sarah called Abraham. They think it sounds like I'm Doug's slave, that he has all the power.

Nope. By "lord," I mean a fine and noble man, worthy of my allegiance. I think of myself as Doug's lady, not his slave, which is probably how Sarah thought since her name means "princess."

What if your husband becomes a tyrant, makes all family decisions on his own or asks you to violate your conscience?

Chapter 6 describes steps you can take. For now, remember that the Bible tells you to treat him as your lord, following him cheerfully and whole-heartedly.

 *Personal Application*

Write a prayer asking God to help you follow your husband's decisions.

Allow him to make mistakes.

I once asked the husbands in a class of newly married couples what they most desired from their wives. The most common response surprised me. It was, "Allow me to make mistakes."

Since your husband is flawed, you can be sure he will make mistakes. When he does, he's likely to be defensive or feel like a failure. Be understanding and supportive, not revengeful. Ask, "Can I help?" instead of saying, "I told you so."

Personal Application

How will you respond when your husband makes a mistake?

Demonstrate Respect

The Bible says, *"The wife must respect her husband" (Ephesians 5:33).* This verse, coming at the end of Paul's famous passage on marriage (Ephesians 5:21-33), has always fascinated me. Paul did not write, "The wife should respect her husband when he earns it." Instead, he said she "must" respect her husband.

This is more important than you might guess. Being a servant-leader is tough. I think that deep down inside, every man who tries to be one fears he isn't doing as good a job as he should. Let your husband know you respect him as your leader and appreciate the things he does. You may be surprised at how much your spouse needs your respect, no matter how gruff or self-sufficient he seems.

Skeeter's note: Doug says the heart of this chapter is that men need the deep respect of their wives—something few of them get.

I once experienced the effect of my respect for Doug in a strange situation: We were at a video arcade and he was playing a video game. His scores were much higher when I watched than when I didn't.

The knights of old went into battle with their lady's scarf floating from their helmet. Men today still prize our assurance that our hearts are with them in their struggles.

"But he hasn't earned my respect."

Sarah voiced a common dilemma when she told me, "The problem is that I don't respect him. How can I show him something I don't feel? I won't lie."

If you face a similar quandary, try the following ideas (borrowed from the third book in this series, *Encouraging Your Spouse*).

- **Show respect because God commands it.**
  A good starting point is to show respect because God said to. The same principle applies to other relationships. For example, Peter wrote we should show respect to everyone and honor the king, although the king in those days was an evil person (1 Peter 2:17).

- **Respect your husband because of his position.**
  You can respect your husband because of his position. For example, after David killed Goliath, he became more popular than King Saul. Saul became jealous and sought to kill David, so David fled. Saul gathered his army and chased David. On two different occasions, when Saul's army was pursuing David, David had the chance to kill Saul.
  Most of us would say that David had every right to kill Saul. After all, Saul was trying to kill him. Yet although he knew that Saul's actions did not deserve respect, David honored Saul as his king and refused to murder him. At his second opportunity to kill Saul, David said, *"The LORD forbid that I should lay a hand on the LORD'S anointed" (1 Samuel 26:11).*
  David respected Saul because of his position. Likewise, respect your husband because of his position.

- **Acknowledge that your husband has weaknesses.**
  Everyone is imperfect. Be careful not to let your spouse's failures erode your respect for his good qualities.

- **Look for things that you can respect.**
  You can find some things your husband does that deserve respect if you look hard enough.

- **Respect your Christian spouse as a child of God.**
  If you are married to a Christian, you are married to one of God's children and should honor him accordingly—regardless of how he is acting. (If you are married to a non-Christian, respect is still necessary for the other reasons listed in this section.)

- **Respect him as made in the image of God.**

  The Bible says, *"In the image of God has God made man" (Genesis 9:6).* Whether or not your husband is a Christian, honor him as God's creation.

- **Honor your husband because God loves him.**

  The Bible says, *"This is love: not that we loved God, but that he loved us and sent his Son as an atoning sacrifice for our sins" (1 John 4:10).* Do not dishonor someone God loves.

- **Respect your mate's desire to be a good person.**

  Your husband may make foolish decisions, eat with bad manners and forget to make the bed. He may be lazy and forgetful. Yet chances are good he wants to be a good person and do the right thing. You can respect the desire of his heart, even if you are disappointed by his actions.

- **Honor your husband for his potential.**

  See your mate as God does. Each of us has an amazing potential. Gideon was a fearful man, living hidden from the enemy, yet the angel of the Lord greeted him, *"The Lord is with you, mighty warrior" (Judges 6:12).* The angel's greeting was not because of anything Gideon had done, but because he knew how God planned to use Gideon.

 *Personal Application*

Write any insights from the above list that will help you respect your husband.

Ask your husband, "What do I do that shows you I respect you?" Write his answer here.

Ask your husband, "What could I do to more clearly show you respect?" Write his answer here.

Honor him above all other people.

Do not treat your parents, children, brothers, sisters or anybody else as more important than your husband. Make sure he knows that he is the most important person in your life.

> *Listen, O daughter, consider and give ear: Forget your people and your father's house. The king is enthralled by your beauty; honor him, for he is your lord (Psalm 45:10-11).*

Learn from him.

God often speaks to people through leaders. Although your husband is not infallible, he is the leader in your partnership and knows you in a special way. Ask his advice. Pay attention to what he says.

Of course, the quality of your husband's guidance will depend to some degree on how well he knows the Bible and how much fruit he bears as a Christian (Galatians 5:22-23). Yet even if he is an unbeliever and has never opened a Bible, he will sometimes have wise words.

Not everything he says will be right. Nonetheless, do not take his words lightly. Consider them. Pray about them. Weigh them according to biblical truths.

Even in matters of doctrine, seek your husband's opinion. His word is not the final authority, for God has given you the Bible and his Holy Spirit. Nonetheless, you can learn from your husband's insights. Read the words of Paul:

> *If they want to inquire about something, they should ask their own husbands at home; for it is disgraceful for a woman to speak in the church (1 Corinthians 14:35).*

These instructions do not mean women must be silent in church (Luke 2:36-38 and 1 Corinthians 11:5), yet they illus-

trate an important principle: Your husband is a gift from God.
Take advantage of this gift.

> *Skeeter's note: I have learned that the flash of an-*
> *noyance I sometimes feel when Doug gives me advice*
> *means he's speaking truth and I don't like it. I used to*
> *think it meant he was wrong.*
>   *I have stewed over some things for years, only to fi-*
> *nally see that I should take Doug's advice. Now,*
> *because of Doug's advice, I am about to finish my first*
> *novel. I was unable to give myself the luxury of writing it*
> *until he said he knew it was God's task for me.*
>   *He takes my advice too.*

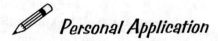 **Personal Application**

List two insights your husband has given you about
yourself.

1.

2.

Is there anything he consistently advises you to do that you haven't done? What is it? Why haven't you?

Do not gossip.

When Billie was with her husband, she seemed like the perfect wife. People watching and listening were struck with her gentle, submissive manner. Yet when she was away from him, her real attitude came out. She belittled him and questioned the sincerity of his faith to anyone who would listen. Skeeter tells me this is not unusual; many women ridicule absent husbands. Let's see what the Bible says about gossip, whether done by a man or a woman:

A gossip betrays a confidence, but a trustworthy man keeps a secret (Proverbs 11:13).

Besides, they get into the habit of being idle and going about from house to house. And not only do they become idlers, but also gossips and busybodies, saying things they ought not to (1 Timothy 5:13).

If you are having marriage problems, it is okay to seek counsel from your pastor, your pastor's spouse, a biblical counselor or one or two mature Christian friends of the same sex. If you request help, ask for prayer and advice about how *you* should act. Do not simply gossip or complain.

 *Personal Application*

Do you sometimes gossip about your husband?
❑ Yes ❑ No

If you do, how will you avoid doing so again?

Be His Helper

"The LORD God said, 'It is not good for the man to be alone. I will make a helper suitable for him'" (Genesis 2:18). Woman's original purpose was to be a helper and friend for man. Adam *needed* Eve and your husband needs you. Each day, pray for him, encourage him and ask yourself, "What can I do to help my husband today?" Be like the wife of noble

character, whose husband *"lacks nothing of value" (Proverbs 31:11).*

Skeeter helps me by praying for me, encouraging me and praising me. She helps me by supporting my dreams, giving me counsel and gently confronting me. She helps me by editing my books, fearlessly slashing my long, cumbersome sentences into something easier to read. She supports me by speaking well of me wherever she goes.

> *Skeeter's note: My main problem here is getting so busy and rut-bound that I neglect to think about ways to help Doug. Is he working too hard? Does he need to take a break? Is he being too strong about everything when he needs me to hold him close and comfort him?*
>
> *I also need to watch the little things: Does he need more socks? Does his tie match his shirt? Is he getting enough wholesome food to eat? Does his hair need cutting?*

You too can make a tremendous difference in your husband's life by helping him. As you seek to be a good helper, bear these cautions in mind:

- Also develop your own gifts and ministries. God has plans for you. Plus, the stronger you are, the more you have to offer your husband.

- Do not try to do everything for your husband. This would not be wise for you or him. Talk with him. Prioritize. Do what matters most.

- Do not take full responsibility for his happiness. Serve him enthusiastically, yet realize that his ultimate joy and peace depend upon his relationship with the Lord.

Personal Application

List three of your husband's goals and interests.

1.

2.

3.

List three things he finds difficult or frustrating.

1.

2.

3.

Write some ways you can help him achieve his goals and overcome his frustrations.

Love Him

Some teach that the Bible says husbands must love their wives, but wives are not required to love their husbands. Nonsense. Jesus said the second greatest commandment is to *"love your neighbor as yourself" (Mark 12:31)*. Your husband is your closest neighbor.

Paul addressed this point when he wrote, *"Likewise, teach the older women to ... train the younger women to love their husbands" (Titus 2:3-4)*.

When Skeeter lets me know she loves me, I am encouraged and strengthened. I thrive on her love. Let your husband know you love him, so he can thrive too.

 *Personal Application*

Learn your husband's "language of love." Ask him three things you do that show him your love.

1.

2.

3.

Write your plans to show him love today and tomorrow.

Putting It All Together

Key point: Respect and follow your husband as your leader.

•

Memory verse: *"Wives, submit to your husbands, as is fitting in the Lord" (Colossians 3:18).*

 *Action Plan*

Choose one or two things from this chapter to work on this week.

1.

2.

Chapter 4

Make Decisions as a Couple

*Plans fail for lack of counsel, but with many advisers
they succeed (Proverbs 15:22).*

How do you and your spouse make decisions? Do you deal
with problems or do you ignore them? Do you work effectively as a team or does one of you take over? Do you talk
courteously or are you unable to talk without arguing?

When you make a decision—whether it is where to go on
vacation or how to deal with a disobedient child—you have
an opportunity to strengthen or weaken your marriage. At
these times, you're doing more than just making a decision.
You're defining your relationship. The decision itself may be
of greater or lesser importance. But how you go about making
it either increases or chips away at your love and sense of
unity.

Read the following points to evaluate your decision-
making style, rating yourselves as a team from 0 to 10 on each
point.

- "0" means, "We don't do this well."
- "10" means, "We are very good at this."

Our score (0-10)

We both are willing to talk about tough issues. .... _____
We both actively participate in discussions .... _____

Neither tries to be domineering. .... _____
Each shows respect for the other's ideas. .... _____
We can disagree without quarreling. .... _____
We usually come to a resolution or make a plan. .... _____
We usually agree on the resolution or plan. .... _____

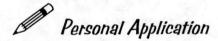 *Personal Application*

Who do you think usually makes decisions in your family?

Describe how you and your spouse make decisions.

Now ask your spouse the same questions and write what he or she thinks here. (Don't be surprised if your mate's answers are different from yours!)

Who my spouse thinks usually makes our decisions:

How my spouse describes our decision-making process:

Face Problems and Make Decisions

I don't like to think about painful problems. I hate tension and I dislike spending money to fix anything. If I could get away with it, I think my motto would be, "Why do it if you can put it off?" Yet I've learned that in the long run, things work out better when I deal with tough issues instead of running from them.

When you don't face problems, you drift through life, letting circumstances or other people make decisions for you. Problems mount higher and become crises. Discouragement turns into hopelessness.

How about you? Do you avoid tough talks? If so, it may be because you feel exhausted or overwhelmed. Perhaps you are married to a domineering spouse, are afraid of arguments or don't want to take responsibility for decisions. Maybe you feel sorry for yourself or think you aren't very smart.

Whatever the reason, it's not a good one. Give your fear and anxiety to God. He is with you and loves you. He will help you make a way.

Cast all your anxiety on him because he cares for you (1 Peter 5:7).

 *Personal Application*

Do you sometimes avoid talking about difficult topics? If so, what are some subjects you do not want to discuss?

What are your techniques for avoiding these conversations?

When you avoid talking about them, what is the message your spouse thinks you are sending?

Write a plan to bring up and discuss one subject in the coming week. Then keep reading to learn how to talk about it.

Set a date and time to talk.

When we delay decisions, we often think we're taking the easy way out, but putting things off usually causes more problems. One couple who saw me for counseling put off deciding about painting their house for years. By the time they took action, the paint was peeling off and some wood siding was damaged.

 *Personal Application*

In the last "Personal Application" question, you identified one subject to discuss. Now talk with your spouse to plan when you will have this discussion.

We agree to talk on (date) _____ at (time) _____.

_____

Practice Teamwork

The key to making decisions is to make them as a team. Nearly all solutions should be agreed upon by both of you as you *"submit to one another" (Ephesians 5:21)*. Do not approach decision-making determined to do things your way. If either one takes over, your one flesh relationship is out of balance and there will be negative results.

Never make a major move such as changing jobs, moving or buying a house without first talking together. In the vast majority of cases, do not make an important decision until both agree.

Follow the same principle with other decisions that affect both of you. For example, don't invite someone to dinner without first getting your mate's okay—unless you previously gave each other permission to make spontaneous invitations. Don't try to get around this by making a tentative invitation and then saying, "I'll have to check with my spouse." If you do this, your spouse may feel pressured to say "yes" to be polite.

Learning how to make decisions as a team is not easy for most of us. We each have our own way of doing things. It's even harder if you are a supervisor at work. You may be used to making decisions and expect your mate to go along. Learning to work as a team may take years of practice. Yet it pays off in big ways.

Team decisions usually are better decisions.

God has given you and your spouse different abilities and experiences. When you work together, you often discover a plan that is better than what either of you could devise alone.

You might say, "That's not true for us. I make great decisions by myself. But when we talk, we never get anywhere." Or, "It takes too long to make decisions together. I could decide what to do in a minute."

If these words describe you, keep reading. Although it may seem like a lot of work, it's important to learn how to make decisions as a team. Two reasons this is true:

- **Two are better than one.**

    Even if you are wise and decisive, you sometimes don't see the whole picture, nor can you think of all the possible solutions to a problem. When you and your spouse learn how to function well together, you increase the brainpower, creativity and prayers you can bring to bear on an issue.

- **Good decision-making strengthens your marriage.**
  When you work through a problem together and come to a joint decision, you increase the sense of unity, love and mutual respect in your marriage. Your one flesh relationship becomes healthier and stronger.

A tragic example of not working as a team can be seen in the story of Nabal and his wife Abigail (1 Samuel 25). Nabal, faced with a difficult situation, reacted in anger and haste. He didn't talk with his wife and made a foolish decision. Had he consulted with her and heeded her advice, he would have lived a longer life.

 Plans fail for lack of counsel, but with many advisers they succeed (Proverbs 15:22).

Participate in discussions.

When you talk with your mate, get involved in the discussion. Don't leave all the decisions, little ones as well as big ones, up to him or her. If you don't participate, your mate may feel abandoned or unloved. You, on the other hand, are likely to resent decisions your spouse makes without you.

I used to say, "I don't care," or, "Whatever you want," when Skeeter asked what I wanted for dinner, which restaurant I'd like to go to or what movie I wanted to see. I thought I was being loving and flexible, but she thought I didn't care enough to put any thought into our marriage. Now I think and give her an answer.

If your mate is domineering and wants to make decisions on his or her own, set up a time to talk. Explain that you would like to make decisions as partners and suggest studying this chapter together. If he or she is not willing to talk, see Chapter 6 for more guidelines.

✐ *Personal Application*

If you rarely participate in decision-making, it may be difficult to change your patterns. Talk with your spouse to plan how you will become more involved. Write your plan here.

_____

Invite your mate to participate.

If your spouse avoids participating in decision-making, politely say that you value his or her opinions and would like to hear them. Request suggestions. Ask questions.

Ask your mate if you do something that makes him or her reluctant to talk. For example, if you usually respond to suggestions by saying, "That's stupid," it's easy to see why your spouse might not want to talk.

If you have been domineering, insisting on doing things your way, ask your spouse to forgive you and make plans to include him or her as an equal partner in your decision-making.

Personal Application

Ask your spouse if you do anything that makes it hard for him or her to talk about decisions. Check the appropriate box. ❑ Yes ❑ No

If the answer is "yes," ask what you could do to improve and write the answer here.

Turn to God

God calls you and your spouse to follow his leadership. Make it your primary goal to honor the Lord in all your decisions.

Unless the Lord builds the house, its builders labor in vain (Psalm 127:1).

Pray together before and after making decisions.

You may have the habit of praying before eating. That's a wonderful tradition and follows Christ's example (Matthew 26:26; Luke 24:30).

Perhaps you already have developed another habit—that of praying before and after making decisions. If you haven't, make it a practice to always pray in your heart to God. In addition, invite your mate to pray with you.

Again, I tell you that if two of you on earth agree about anything you ask for, it will be done for you by my Father in heaven. For where two or three come together in my name, there am I with them (Matthew 18:19-20).

Devote yourselves to prayer, being watchful and thankful (Colossians 4:2).

Look to God's Word.

Study the Bible to make sure you follow God's commands and principles when making decisions. Be like the psalmist who wrote, *"I have hidden your word in my heart that I might not sin against you" (Psalm 119:11).*

Do not let this Book of the Law depart from your mouth; meditate on it day and night, so that you may be careful to do everything written in it. Then you will be prosperous and successful (Joshua 1:8).

The grass withers and the flowers fall, but the word of our God stands forever (Isaiah 40:8).

Do not violate either person's conscience.

Don't take any steps that would violate either person's conscience, even if the action is not directly addressed in the Scriptures.

As one who is in the Lord Jesus, I am fully convinced that no food is unclean in itself. But if

anyone regards something as unclean, then for him it is unclean. ... But the man who has doubts is condemned if he eats, because his eating is not from faith; and everything that does not come from faith is sin (Romans 14:14, 23).

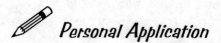 **Personal Application**

Before making important decisions, we pray together:

<u>0   1   2   3   4   5   6   7   8   9   10</u>
Never   Always

Talk with your spouse and agree to pray together when you make important decisions.

❏ We agree to pray about important decisions.

Communicate Courteously

Over the years, you will make hundreds of decisions. When you look back at the end of your life, you will realize most of them were not as important as you thought at the time. You will also see that the way you made the decisions either drew you closer together or pushed you apart. Your courtesy, or lack of it, usually is more important than the actual decision. True wisdom is peace-loving.

 But the wisdom that comes from heaven is first of all pure; then peace-loving, considerate,

submissive, full of mercy and good fruit, impartial and sincere. Peacemakers who sow in peace raise a harvest of righteousness (James 3:17-18).

Speak respectfully and politely.

Do not speak down to your mate, but as one adult to another. Avoid sarcasm and anger. Instead, make your words things of beauty, *"like apples of gold in settings of silver"* *(Proverbs 25:11).*

 Words from a wise man's mouth are gracious, but a fool is consumed by his own lips (Ecclesiastes 10:12).

Really listen to your mate.

Do not assume you are right or there is only one correct way to do something. Your spouse may have a better idea. Or the two of you together may come up with an entirely different solution.

 The way of a fool seems right to him, but a wise man listens to advice (Proverbs 12:15).

Pride only breeds quarrels, but wisdom is found in those who take advice (Proverbs 13:10).

Listen to advice and accept instruction, and in the end you will be wise (Proverbs 19:20).

Do not give in to anger.

Decisions made in anger usually are poor decisions since *"man's anger does not bring about the righteous life that God desires" (James 1:20).* Wait until both of you calm down before making a decision.

Dig deeper if you need help to speak courteously.

If you need further help, Book 5 in this series, *Talking with Respect and Love,* is full of practical, biblical advice that can help you communicate courteously and effectively.

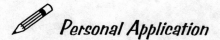 *Personal Application*

Select one area in which you would like to improve:

❑ Speaking respectfully and politely
❑ Really listening to my mate
❑ Not giving in to anger

Now ask your spouse for suggestions about how you can improve in this area. Write his or her ideas here.

Consider What's Best for Your Mate

The Bible says to *"look not only to your own interests, but also to the interests of others" (Philippians 2:3-4).* Rather than trying to get what you want, defer to your mate. At times, this will mean saying, "I don't see it like you do, but let's do it your way."

However, notice that Paul wrote *"not only."* It is okay to consider your own interests sometimes, as long as you are primarily concerned for your spouse.

 *Personal Application*

When talking about decisions, do you usually think first about what would be best for your spouse?
❏ Yes ❏ No

Think about the last few decisions you and your spouse made. *When you talked, were you mainly thinking about your interests or your spouse's interests?* If you think you were equally concerned with each of your interests, check both boxes.

The decision: _____
    ❏ My interests ❏ My spouse's interests

The decision: _____
    ❏ My interests ❏ My spouse's interests

The decision: _____
    ❏ My interests ❏ My spouse's interests

Go to the Bible: For the next two weeks, read Philippians 2:1-21 every morning and pray for a servant's heart.

Use Wisdom

Many of our decisions are based on emotions. Although that is appropriate sometimes, it isn't at other times. The type of car you buy, where you send your children to school, how you spend your spare time and which church you attend all involve your emotions, yet these decisions also require prayer and logical analysis. The following guidelines can help you make wise decisions.

Pray.

Ask God to help you make a decision that pleases him. Also ask for grace to talk with love and respect.

Define the issue you are discussing.

After praying for God's help, define what you are talking about. If you are trying to resolve a problem:

- **Identify underlying problems.**

  The original issue may be, "We never go on dates." As you talk, you may discover underlying problems, such as, "We both take on too many obligations."

- **Identify your part.**

  When you talk, it may be necessary to talk about frustrations you have with your mate. However, remember to focus first on how you contributed to the problem.

 You hypocrite, first take the plank out of your own eye, and then you will see clearly to remove the speck from your brother's eye (Matthew 7:5).

Identify possible plans.

Talk together to come up with a list of things you could do. The first idea one of you comes up with may not be the best idea.

Do not just complain. If you say, "We never have any fun," suggest activities you both enjoy. Make a list. Ask if your spouse would like to do any of these things. Invite him or her to make suggestions.

Evaluate the options.

Once you make a list of possible solutions, evaluate each one. Discuss the ideas without ridicule or condemnation. Explore possibilities. Seek a solution with which you both feel comfortable.

Even if you do not like any of the choices you identify, choose the best one unless you can afford to wait and discuss the situation again.

Decide if one of you should have a greater voice.

Sometimes it makes sense to pay more attention to the opinion of one spouse or the other. The following guidelines are not laws; there may be times when other factors should come into play.

- **Recognize areas of expertise.**

   If either of you has more knowledge or expertise in the area under discussion, take advantage of this knowledge. Yet do not discount the other person's opinions.

   Skeeter knows much more about plants than I do, so I gladly let her make most landscaping decisions. Yet I would not simply go along if she wanted to plant a cornfield in the front yard.

- **Ask who cares the most about the decision.**

   If something is very important to one person and not to the other, it may make sense for that person to have the greater say in the decision. Skeeter and I sometimes identify how important something is to each of us by rating its significance on a scale of 0 to 10.

- **Look at whom the decision will affect the most.**
  Sometimes it is reasonable for the person who is most affected by a decision to have the greatest say. This principle often holds true in decisions about time. For example, if you would like your wife to home school your children, give her the greatest say in the decision, since she would do most of the teaching.

- **Do not make decisions for your spouse.**
  Allow your spouse to make decisions that primarily affect him or her. If your mate is thinking about enrolling in a gardening class, feel free to discuss it, but let him or her make the decision.

Take turns making some types of decisions.

One way to decide whom to invite for dinner, what movie to see or where to go on a vacation is to take turns. If one person usually makes the decisions, this will help the passive spouse get involved.

Seek the advice of others.

If you cannot agree, it may be wise to ask your pastor or a mature Christian friend for advice. This may be humbling, yet it could help you discover the best possible solution.

 For lack of guidance a nation falls, but many advisers make victory sure (Proverbs 11:14).

Make the decision as a team.

As I have written throughout this book, make a decision you both feel comfortable with.

Clarify your decision.

Once you decide, be sure each of you understands your decision. It is common for two people to walk away from a discussion with radically different ideas about the outcome. Be clear about each person's responsibilities to carry out your plan.

Likewise, make sure that a real decision has been made before you take action. If you say you would like to paint the house, and your spouse says, "That's a good idea," or, "Maybe I could go for that," do not assume a thumbs up. Your mate's comment might only mean he or she is open to further discussion. Be sure you have an agreed-upon plan before buying paint.

Pray.

When you are done talking, pray together for God's blessing upon the decision. Also pray for peace between yourselves if you felt any tension as you talked.

 *Personal Application*

How would your decision-making as a couple improve if you followed the above steps?

Do you need to put more effort into practicing any of the above guidelines? If so, which ones?

At Times the Husband Must Decide

Although marriage is a partnership, the husband is the head and on occasion may need to make a final decision. He should take this step rarely, always being careful to be courteous and respectful. When he does, his wife should graciously follow his leadership.

Note to the husband

Remember that you are called to be a servant to your wife, not a big shot. Discuss issues and seek mutual decisions. If you think you need to take action on your own, be sure you have been walking in the Spirit and have bathed the decision in love and prayer.

Be careful! In my experience, when men make "executive decisions," they usually have not truly tried to make a decision as a couple.

When you make a decision, be clear about what it is so there will be no confusion. Communicate it politely and respectfully.

Once you have done so, you have done your duty. It is now up to your wife to follow your leadership. You are not responsible to bring her into submission. Continue to live in a loving relationship with her, regardless of how she responds to your leadership.

Note to the wife

If your husband makes a decision, accept it graciously. Give him the message: "When we talk, I hope we can follow the biblical guidelines in this book and I hope we usually can come to mutual decisions. But when you make a final decision, I will support you."

As you will see in Chapter 6, there are exceptions to this principle. For example, if your husband wants you to violate the Scriptures or your conscience, respectfully refuse.

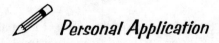 *Personal Application*

Review the above points that apply to you as a husband or wife and then write a brief commitment to follow them.

Be Gracious if a Plan Doesn't Work

How do you respond when you do something the way your husband or wife wanted and it doesn't turn out well? It's okay to talk about it, but do so with love and respect. Never say, "I told you so."

Skeeter and I once faced an investment decision. We did not agree on a course of action, so we decided to do what I thought was best. It turned out to be a bad choice. Once it became clear we had made a mistake, Skeeter was friendly and supportive. We talked about the situation and learned some lessons. She never got angry or rubbed it in.

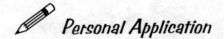 *Personal Application*

How gracious are you when your mate's ideas do not work?

0	1	2	3	4	5	6	7	8	9	10

I am bitter   I am gracious

What will help you be more gracious?

Putting It All Together

Key point: Make decisions as a team, using each person's insights and strengths.

•

Memory verse: *"Plans fail for lack of counsel, but with many advisers they succeed" (Proverbs 15:22).*

 *Action Plan*

Choose one or two things from this chapter to work on this week.

1.

2.

Chapter 5
Practice Teamwork throughout the Day

Two are better than one, because they have a good re-turn for their work (Ecclesiastes 4:9).

The biggest challenges facing a couple are often found in day-to-day living. Once you learn how to make decisions as a team, you still have to figure out how you will divide the work of earning a living, raising children, doing household chores, paying the bills, maintaining the car and taking care of hundreds of other details of life.

Before we look at guidelines for dividing the labor, let's look at three couples who did a poor job of it.

Ronald and Peggy

Ronald worked eight hours a day and his wife Peggy was a full-time homemaker. They had two children. When Ron came home from work, he thought his duties for the day were done. He kissed Peggy, played with the kids for a few minutes, ate dinner and then settled down to an evening of TV.

While Ron relaxed, Peggy was in constant motion, cooking and serving dinner, supervising the children, washing dishes, helping with homework, making sure the kids brushed their teeth, saying prayers with them and then picking up around the house.

Ron was vaguely aware that Peggy was working hard, but thought it was her duty. He had put in an eight-hour day, after all, and deserved a break. It never crossed his mind that Peggy, too, had put in a full day's work by the time he came home. The result: Peggy worked a lot more than Ron.

Ben and Shirley

Ben also worked at an eight-hours-a-day job. He and Shirley had no children. While he worked, she spent most of the day shopping, reading, talking with friends and watching TV.

Shirley expected Ben to provide for her financially, thinking that was the man's job, but she completely rejected the old-fashioned idea that she should clean the house, cook or wash the dishes. Instead, she thought, housework should be a 50-50 proposition. Every night Ben came home to a mess and then helped cook and clean house. The result: Ben worked a lot more than Shirley.

Jim and Robin

Jim and Robin did not have children and each had a full-time job. Jim had strong ideas about "man's work" and "woman's work." When home, he did the yard work, maintained the cars and occasionally barbecued chicken for dinner. Robin was left with cooking, cleaning and doing most other household tasks. The result: Robin worked a lot more than Jim.

 *Personal Application*

Think of all the work it takes to earn a living, raise children and run a household. Do you think you do your fair share? ❏ Yes ❏ No

What is the division of labor in your marriage? How well
does it work?

The Wife is the Main Homemaker

In both the Old and New Testaments, the Bible portrays
the wife as the primary homemaker. Although there are many
different ways a couple can divide the labor, God has given
her the job of establishing a nurturing, Christ-centered environment—a refuge for the couple, a nest for the kids and a
welcoming environment for visitors.

Before looking at what this means in practice, let's look at
some Scriptures. Proverbs 31:10-31 is a good place to start. In
this passage, we read about the *"wife of noble character"*
(verse 10), a woman who manages her family's daily activities, yet is also active in the world of commerce.

She is in charge of *"her servant girls" (verse 15)* and
"watches over the affairs of her household" (verse 27). The
Hebrew word translated as "watches over" means she ob-
serves her household, or keeps watch.

This woman *"provides food for her family" (verse 15).* She *"makes coverings for her bed" (verse 22)* and *"does not eat the bread of idleness" (verse 27).* Because of this, *"Her children arise and call her blessed; her husband also, and he praises her" (verse 28).*

Paul addressed the wife's role when he wrote that wives are to be *"busy at home" (Titus 2:5).* The New American Standard Bible translates the same passage by saying wives are to be *"workers at home."* The King James Bible says they are to be *"keepers at home."* The Greek word that is translated these three ways means they are to stay home and be good housekeepers.

Paul also referred to the wife's duty to manage or guide the home in his first letter to Timothy:

> *So I counsel younger widows to marry, to have children, to manage their homes and to give the enemy no opportunity for slander (1 Timothy 5:14).*

Personal Application

How do you react to these verses?

The value of homemaking

Skeeter became a Christian in 1968, followed by me in 1969. Up until then, we had believed in a hodge-podge of hippie/radical/egalitarian/Zen/yoga ideas that sounded good, but which didn't work well in real life.

When we became Christians, we gladly discarded our previous beliefs and embraced what the Bible had to say. Although we made mistakes along the way, Skeeter found the role of homemaker and mother to be extremely rewarding.

Then some time later she began watching a popular weekly TV program for women. The regular message was that homemaking was a waste of a good woman and that women should have careers. As Skeeter watched week after week, this message slowly worked its way into her mind, and she started thinking that maybe she was being cheated out of a meaningful life.

Skeeter still loved our children and me, but she wrestled with dissatisfaction for years. Then, before the boys left home, the desire for a career grew stronger and she got a half time job as a reporter for a small newspaper. A few years later she moved up to writing for a major newspaper. Although this job, too, was halftime, she threw herself into it and worked many unpaid hours.

She is a highly skilled writer and did well, yet after a few years she began to think she was making a mistake by putting in such long hours. Our youngest son, then in high school, was coming home to an empty house, and Skeeter found herself thinking about the missed opportunities to be with him. After a lot of praying she quit, partly so she could see more of him in his last two years at home.

Skeeter still cherishes memories of those after-school visits and wonders how she could have ever sacrificed time with her son just to write another story. She says her biggest mistake was in believing the lie that homemaking is demeaning and that one can only find fulfillment in a career.

Does this mean it was wrong for her to work in the first place? Not necessarily. As you will read, it's not unbiblical for a woman to work. But she made a mistake when she neglected our son to build a career.

Relationships are what really count in life—first, our relationship with God; next, our relationship with our family and last, our relationships with others. It's not that big a deal to win the rat race. Success in a career is insignificant compared to success in a family.

Being a homemaker is of great value to God, a special calling that results in lasting blessings.

What is a home?

What is a home? A mother sews matching Easter dresses for her daughters, working through the night so the dresses will be ready in time. A father fries Saturday morning pancakes, being corny and silly as he cooks.

A child thinks of home: clean sheets, warm food, rain patter on a roof that doesn't leak as he or she lies snug in bed. Prayers before going to school. A band-aid on the "owie." A story made up by Daddy. A lullaby sung by Mommy.

A home is a place you can safely rest, safely laugh, safely cry. Someone always gives you a long hug when you return and wants to know everything that happened to you while you were away. A home can be the grand palace of Solomon or a manger in Bethlehem because it is not the place, but the people in it, that are the home.

To make a good home takes all a mother's intellect, creativity, management expertise, social skills and heart—and the active help of her husband.

She must manage a thousand details—when to get tetanus shots, where soccer practice will be held, the baby's feeding schedule, the cheapest place to buy strawberry jam.

How does she spend her time? She centers her life in the joys and responsibilities of homemaking, yet she may also have an active life that extends into numerous, varied activities. Look at the wife of noble character in Proverbs 31: In addition to homemaking, she engaged in commerce and helped the poor and needy. She was on the go.

The husband should respect the wife's position.

Men, honor your wife's work as a homemaker, whether she is at home fulltime or part-time. It is a profession that receives much too little respect.

I don't think I will ever forget the tears of a woman who, as part of a panel of four wives, shared her heart at church on Mother's Day. She cried as she talked, describing how little support she received as a full-time homemaker, even from other women in the church.

Never joke about your wife being "just" a homemaker. Likewise, don't insult her by saying you have a "real" job and she doesn't. If your wife wants to stay home to raise the kids, try to make that happen. Do not push her to get an outside job unless it is absolutely necessary.

What about the husband's headship?

Men, as you saw in chapters 2 and 3, you have the primary leadership role in your home, yet you are to be a servant-leader and must be submitted to God. Be involved in the family and provide oversight over what's going on, but remember that homemaking is your wife's job. Do not micromanage her, pointing out mistakes or telling her how to do everything.

Give her lots of praise and only occasional suggestions. Ask yourself how you would feel if someone looked over your shoulder and kept criticizing you on your job. You wouldn't like it.

Men, too, should not get too caught up in a career.

Don't put too much time and effort into your career. Work is honorable, and God expects you to do it well. But do not base your identity on your career. Your relationship with God and your family are much more important and much more lasting. Many men live with deep regrets because they spent so much time on the job that they did not develop an intimate oneness with their wife and friendship with their children.

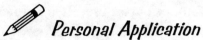 *Personal Application*

Do you need to reexamine your priorities?
❑ Yes ❑ No

What changes do you need to make in attitude and action?

Changes in attitude:

Changes in action:

Who Should Earn Money?

Since the Bible instructs the wife to be busy as a home-maker, the primary responsibility to earn a living falls upon the husband. This is the pattern in most marriages described in the Bible.

However, the Scriptures also tell of women who helped provide for their families' needs. For example, Acts 18:2-3 refers to Priscilla, a woman who helped her husband make tents.

Likewise, we read about the wife of noble character in Proverbs 31. She managed her home but also was a business-woman. She bought property and planted a vineyard out of her earnings (verse 16), was involved in trading (verse 18) and made and sold garments (verse 24).

We don't know what her husband's income-producing activities were, but it's possible she made more money than he. That's the situation in many modern marriages—both people have jobs, and the wife earns more money. Sometimes this is hard on a man's pride, but it shouldn't be. All that matters is that he works diligently and keeps growing in the Lord.

Mom should be home with young children.

A mother should be as intimately involved in her children's lives as possible and should be home most of the time when the kids are there. Remember that she is to be *"busy at home" (Titus 2:5).* You cannot underestimate the value of a mother raising her children.

However, if she doesn't get stretched too thin, it may be fine for her to also have a part-time or home-based job. Look again at the wife of noble character in Proverbs 31. She was devoted to her children, yet she was also involved in commerce. Since she had servant girls, it is likely those girls cared for her kids from time to time. This would have been similar to a woman hiring a babysitter or putting the children in day-care with trusted friends for a while.

The key is to always place the welfare of the kids first. As I wrote earlier, many women get too caught up in a career and neglect their children. I have counseled thousands of people and have heard heartbreaking stories as many described feeling abandoned as children. And I have heard hair-curling stories of teenage "latchkey" kids having sex in their parents' bed while Dad and Mom were at work.

"Our circumstances don't allow Mom to stay home."

Brenda's husband Frank lost his job. Shortly thereafter, he got cancer and she went to work to keep a roof over their heads. Was there something wrong with that? Of course not. Frank took over as many of the home chores as he could.

There are other reasons mothers work at fulltime jobs and leave major parenting responsibilities to the husband or others. Some examples:

- The wife may support a husband who is going to college.

- The wife may help support her husband as he gets a new business going.

- The wife may support her husband for a year so he can write a book.

- Each person may have to work for the family to survive financially.

If your family is in a similar situation, it may be appropriate for Mom to get a job. However, don't automatically assume this is the best decision. There may be better solutions that allow her to be home with the kids. Many families, for example, could cut back on their standard of living, so Mom doesn't have to work at a fulltime job.

Talk and pray together about your circumstances. If it's necessary for Mom to work fulltime, don't feel guilty. God will help you.

Even if Mom works fulltime, she should keep thinking of ways to make her home more of a home. Little touches can go a long way.

If Mom has a job, Dad needs to pitch in to help with homemaking tasks. I've known many men who expected their wife to hold down a fulltime job and also take care of all the domestic chores. Those husbands needed to improve on their servant's attitude.

Things change as the kids grow older.

Dorothy was married to Curt, a pastor. When their children were at home, she threw herself into making a nest, providing a stimulating, nurturing environment. She did a great job and also had time to help out at church. When the kids grew up and moved out, she became involved in a fulltime ministry. As she said, there is a season for everything.

This transition can start before the children leave home. When they are at school or attend activities throughout the day, the wife certainly shouldn't feel obligated to sit at home alone.

Some husbands feel threatened when the kids leave home. Lyle, for example, had been content when his wife Yolanda was a fulltime homemaker. But he came unglued when the kids left home and she wanted to go back to college. Instead of supporting her, he threw roadblock after roadblock in her way. He was afraid she would meet someone and have an affair.

The harder Lyle held on to Yolanda, the more frustrated she got. It was a struggle for him, but he finally stopped trying to control her and allowed her to develop her God-given gifts. At the same time, he worked on making a better marriage, and they ended up happier than they had ever been.

 *Personal Application*

Who earns the money in your home?

Are you both comfortable with your pattern?
❑ Yes ❑ No

Would you like to see the wife spend more time with the children? ❑ Yes ❑ No

If you would like to make any changes, what would they be?

Share the Workload

If you sit back and let your mate do more than you, you have not grasped the Bible's message about mutual submission. Remember, we are to look for ways to serve, not be served.

Families have different patterns.
The Bible does not portray a single pattern that applies to all families. The ice-skaters I wrote about in Chapter 1 follow certain rules, yet as they follow these rules, there is an infinite number of routines they can perform.

This is also true of marriage. Although the wife is to be the primary homemaker, the Bible does not specify exactly what she is to do, leaving her much freedom to make a unique nest without following a set pattern.

The Bible does not define "man's work" and "woman's work" in the home. It's okay for a woman to change the oil in the car. And it is a good idea for a man to change the baby's diapers.

Ben, a friend of mine, loves to cook, so he prepares dinner. There's nothing wrong with that. But he would be out of line if he tried to prevent his wife from cooking or criticized her when she did.

The way your family works depends on many circumstances, such as:

- Who works how long outside the home

- How many children you have and their ages

- The health of each person

- Outside commitments such as helping sick parents

- Your individual skills and interests

Regardless of your marriage's pattern, do not slip into the habit of viewing your mate as your personal servant. Clean up your own messes and pick up your dirty clothes.

Do more than your share.

Do you remember the three couples at the beginning of this chapter? In each family, one person carried a much heavier load, which is unfair. Whatever the division of labor in your marriage, each should strive to do more than his or her half of the work.

On the other hand, if you think things are way out of balance, it's okay to express your concern. The next chapter discusses how to do so.

 *Personal Application*

Write a prayer asking God to help you be willing to do more than 50 percent of the work.

Define responsibilities.

Talk with your spouse about how the work is shared in your marriage. Don't assume anything is "woman's work" or "man's work." Work is work, and it needs to be done.

Look at the example of Jesus. Although he was God with us, he performed servant's work as he washed his disciples' feet. When he was done, he said, *"I have set you an example that you should do as I have done for you" (John 13:15).*

After you divide the labor, do not insist that your mate do things your way. If he or she loads the dishwasher differently than you would, don't get upset. Instead, be glad for clean dishes.

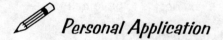 *Personal Application*

Talk with your mate about how you share the labor. Are you both satisfied? Would either like to see changes? When you talk, cover such things as:

Earning money	Raising kids	Paying bills
Cleaning house	Cooking	Gardening
Doing home repairs	Writing letters	Shopping

What changes, if any, have you agreed on?

Have weekly planning meetings.

It can be helpful to get together once a week to review how you are doing as a family and make plans for the coming week. When you talk, review your division of labor and how well it is working. You may need to make adjustments.

You could also discuss personal goals at this time. These might include your desires to study the Bible more, grow in love, tell others about Christ or change careers.

 *Personal Application*

Talk with your mate about starting weekly planning meetings. If you decide to have them:

When will you get together?

Where will you meet?

_____

Redefine responsibilities when situations change.

If circumstances change, redefine roles. If someone takes on a second job, he or she probably should do less around the house. If someone retires, he or she should take on more responsibilities.

Help your spouse through hard times.

Make allowances for your mate's life circumstances. He or she may be worn out after a long day or sad because of ailing parents. Perhaps your mate is going through other difficulties. If your mate could use some encouragement, give an extra hug, offer to talk or do some of his or her chores.

Two are better than one, because they have a good return for their work: If one falls down, his friend can help him up. But pity the man who falls and has no one to help him up! Also, if two lie down together, they will keep warm. But how can one keep warm alone? Though one may be over-powered, two can defend themselves. A cord of three strands is not quickly broken (Ecclesiastes 4:9-12).

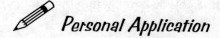

Personal Application

Is your spouse going through a difficult time?
❏ Yes ❏ No

If so, what can you do to help?

Raise Children as a Team

The Bible portrays parenting as a team effort. However, some couples fall into a strict division of labor that is unbiblical and not good for the children. In the following pages, we will look at three areas in which one parent or the other often drops the ball. Before we do that, however, let's look at an underlying principle: the importance of supporting your spouse's parenting.

Support your spouse in front of the kids.

Your children should see the two of you as a team. Do not criticize your spouse to your children. Instead, praise your mate and support him or her in front of the kids.

In general, if you disagree with your spouse, talk behind closed doors. For example:

- **If you disagree with what your mate is doing**

  It is hard to be supportive when you don't like how your spouse is disciplining a child. The desire to intervene may be strong. Yet intervening usually does more harm than good. Your mate becomes upset and your children see you arguing. It is usually better to talk with your spouse later when you are alone.

  Another approach would be for you to agree upon a signal either parent could use when concerned about the other's actions. For example, "Could we all take some time-out now?" Then you could have a private talk.

  If your spouse is physically abusing a child, intervene immediately.

- **If you disagree with what your mate already did**

  If you disagree with the way your husband or wife handled a situation with the kids, it's usually best not to overturn your mate's decision. Instead, talk privately.

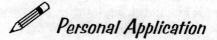

Personal Application

Write any ways in which you have not supported your spouse in front of the children.

How will you support your mate in the future?

Share the responsibility to encourage the children.

Some think that raising children is the mother's job. They do not see fathers as responsible to change diapers or do much of anything as the children grow up.

Although the mother is the primary homemaker, children also need a gentle and nurturing father—not a gruff army drill sergeant. Look at the words Paul used to describe a good father:

For you know that we dealt with each of you as a father deals with his own children, encouraging, comforting and urging you to live lives worthy of God, who calls you into his kingdom and glory (1 Thessalonians 2:11-12).

How nurturing are you? Rate yourself from 0 to 10 on each point. (Note that this quiz is for mothers as well as fathers.)

- "0" means, "I don't do this much at all."
- "10" means, "I do this a lot."

My score (0-10)

I talk with the kids a lot in a friendly way .... _____
I play with them .... _____
I encourage and comfort them .... _____
I supervise them .... _____
I help them learn how to do chores .... _____
I tell them I love them .... _____
I comfort them when they are hurt .... _____
I help with their homework .... _____
I help them prepare for bedtime .... _____
I tell them a nighttime story .... _____
I am patient with them .... _____

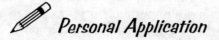 *Personal Application*

Select one point in the above quiz on which you scored yourself seven or lower.

Write three specific ways you will improve on this in the future.

1.

2.

3.

Share the responsibility to provide spiritual training.
Nothing is more important for parents than to introduce
their children to God's Word and to God himself. Yet in many
families, one or both parents fail in this duty. Notice that the
Bible gives both mother and father this responsibility.

*Listen, my son, to your father's instruction
and do not forsake your mother's teaching (Proverbs 1:8).*

*These commandments that I give you today
are to be upon your hearts. Impress them on your
children. Talk about them when you sit at home
and when you walk along the road, when you lie
down and when you get up. Tie them as symbols
on your hands and bind them on your foreheads.
Write them on the doorframes of your houses and
on your gates (Deuteronomy 6:6-9).*

How involved are you with your children's spiritual up-
bringing? Rate yourself from 0 to 10 on each of the following
points.

- "0" means, "I don't do this much at all."
- "10" means, "I do this a lot."

My score (0-10)

I pray with the kids regularly.............................. _____
I talk with them about God throughout the day............ _____
I set a good example with my church attendance......... _____
I help them get ready for church......................... _____
I talk with them about their church activities.............. _____
I take them to special church events....................... _____
I lead family or individual Bible studies..................... _____

Personal Application

Do you need to be more actively involved in your children's spiritual lives?   ☐ Yes   ☐ No

If you answered "yes," write what you will do differently, then pray for God's help to follow through.

Share the responsibility to discipline.

The Bible tells children to obey their parents. It also lets us know obedience does not come naturally. Children need training.

Both parents are called to roles of authority, to train their children to be respectful and obedient. But in many families, one parent—usually the mother—backs away from this role, leaving the other responsible for all discipline. Notice in the following verses that God tells children to obey *both* parents.

Both parents are called to roles of authority, to train their children to be respectful and obedient. But in many families, one parent—usually the mother—backs away from this role, leaving the other one responsible for all discipline. Notice in the following verses that God tells children to obey *both* parents.

> *Children, obey your parents in the Lord, for this is right (Ephesians 6:1).*

> *The rod of correction imparts wisdom, but a child left to himself disgraces his mother (Proverbs 29:15).*

Women who see discipline as the father's responsibility often fear seeming mean and losing their children's love. Sometimes they think they are not emotionally strong enough to deal with a strong-willed child. And sometimes they are actually intimidated by a child. The result? Disrespectful and disobedient children.

Whenever you discipline, do so in love. Chastisement delivered in anger usually has worse results than if you do not chastise at all.

> *Brothers, if someone is caught in a sin, you who are spiritual should restore him gently (Galatians 6:1).*

> *Fathers, do not exasperate your children; instead, bring them up in the training and instruction of the Lord (Ephesians 6:4).*

Personal Application

Do you need to be more authoritative?
☐ Yes ☐ No

If so, what changes will you make?

_____

Strengthen Your Team

This chapter has dealt with sharing the responsibilities involved in day-to-day living. Now let's look at some ways you can strengthen your team.

Spend time together.
After work, talk apart from the kids for a few minutes. Discuss how your day went. Briefly pray together. Make plans for the evening.

Also schedule times to go on walks, eat dinner at a restaurant or go on other dates. Don't get so caught up in day-to-day chores or raising kids that you do not take the time to build your friendship.

Face the world as a team.

Let others know you are a team. Praise your mate when with others. Do not gossip about your husband or wife.

If a friend says he or she wants to tell me something in confidence, I usually say that since Skeeter and I are a team, I won't keep a secret from her. (However, when I see people as a counselor, I respect their confidentiality.) Skeeter almost always says the same thing when others want to tell her secrets.

We even consider mail sent to one as sent to both. Each of us feels free to read letters or e-mails sent to the other. We don't think of this as snooping. We think of this as being one flesh.

We do have some exceptions to our policy of openness. As I just wrote, I don't tell Skeeter things people tell me when counseling and I don't read entries she writes in her private journal.

Learn from your mate.

Skeeter knows me better than anyone else, so she is a great source of feedback. The first several years I taught adult Bible classes in our church, I asked her for suggestions at the end of each class. She usually had quite a few, saying I should speak more slowly, use more examples, walk around more and avoid clichés. I was humbled on many occasions, but I became a better teacher.

Likewise, each of us learned a lot about raising children from the other. I became more nurturing as a result of Skeeter's comments. She became more comfortable with control and discipline because of my suggestions.

Personal Application

Review the above suggestions for strengthening your teamwork. Write any ways you would like to implement them in your marriage.

Putting It All Together

Key point: Share the load, each doing more than his or her share. Allow the wife to be the chief homemaker.

•

Memory verse: *"Two are better than one, because they have a good return for their work" (Ecclesiastes 4:9).*

 *Action Plan*

Choose one or two things from this chapter to work on this week.

1.

2.

Chapter 6

Overcome Partnership Problems

As iron sharpens iron, so one man sharpens another (Proverbs 27:17).

What happens when your teamwork breaks down? In this chapter, you will read many problems and solutions, most drawn from my counseling experience. If you face something that is not discussed, look for principles you can apply in your circumstances.

You will see that many of the solutions involve talking about the problems. These discussions are difficult, yet when done in love, they can be life-giving.

 The wise in heart are called discerning, and pleasant words promote instruction (Proverbs 16:21).

Better is open rebuke than hidden love. Wounds from a friend can be trusted, but an enemy multiplies kisses (Proverbs 27:5-6).

Now, before going further, take a deep breath and say a brief prayer. Reading about these problems can be depressing! But be encouraged. For every problem there is a solution.

Deal with a Controlling Mate

In some marriages, the husband tries to dominate his wife. In others, the wife tries to take over—or each tries to control the other. The following guidelines are written for a woman who is married to a controlling husband. However, most of these guidelines also apply to a husband who is married to a controlling wife.

"My husband is domineering."

Do you think your husband is demanding or controlling? Does he speak disrespectfully to you? Before talking to him about this, evaluate yourself. Do you give him a message of respect, or do you constantly attack or criticize him? Do you acknowledge him as your head, or do you make a battle out of everything? Ask the Lord about changes *you* should make (Matthew 7:1-5). Then talk with your husband.

- **If he demands too much of you**

    Reassure him that you want to be a good wife, but cannot do *everything* he wants. Ask him to prioritize his desires.

- **If he orders you around**

    Let him know you acknowledge him as your head, but point out times when he constantly tells you what to do or treats you like a child. Politely refuse if he says you can't go to church or tells you to disobey God in other ways (Exodus 1:17; Acts 4:19-20; Acts 5:29). Likewise, say "no" if he wants you to violate your conscience (1 Timothy 1:5, 19; 1 Peter 3:16).

- **If he forbids you to see family or friends**

    From time to time, I hear of a wife whose husband forbids her to visit her parents or certain friends. If you're in that situation, first try to understand why he is concerned. It may be that you have put your parents and friends before him. Or some of your friends may be influencing you to turn away from God.

Let him know you will think about his concerns. Be open to the possibility that you should cut back on contacts with certain people. Yet also let him know he is going too far by making demands, especially if he tells you not to see your parents. The Bible refers to leaving parents (Genesis 2:24), but that doesn't mean never seeing them. Ordering your wife not to see them would be asking her to violate Scriptures that tell us to honor our parents (Exodus 20:12; Matthew 15:3-6).

- **If he frequently gets angry**

    Lovingly but firmly set limits if he yells at you or confronts you in anger. Explain that you are willing to talk about anything, but only if you both talk courteously. If the anger continues, call "time-out." Ask your pastor for help.

"My husband says I'm not submissive."

Along the same lines, if your husband says he doesn't think you have a submissive attitude, don't respond with anger or defensiveness. Instead, ask what he means. It's possible that he is right. It's also possible that he is wrong.

Prayerfully search your heart. If you think he is right, apologize, ask his forgiveness and seek God's help to change. On the other hand, if your husband has misread you, gently reassure him.

"I have been a doormat, not a wife."

If you have been submissive in an unhealthy way, feeling worthless or timid, review Chapter 3, especially the section on "Serve from Strength." Then talk with your husband. Let him know how your misunderstanding of submission has weakened your marriage by making you a lesser partner than you could have been. Tell him you plan to become a stronger, yet still submissive, wife. Ask for his help in this project.

If he does not want you to change, respectfully and lovingly ask him to read this book. Even if he does not change his attitude, look at yourself with new eyes, as a strong woman with gifts from God. Don't continue to bury your talents. Be submissive, but in a new, more balanced way.

"My wife is domineering."

As I wrote at the beginning of this section, sometimes it is the wife who is controlling, not the husband. If you are married to a domineering wife, most of the above guidelines also apply to your situation.

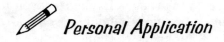 *Personal Application*

Do you think your spouse is controlling? ❑ Yes ❑ No

If you checked "yes," have you encouraged this behavior in any way? If so, how?

What steps should you take?

Do not Tolerate Physical Abuse

In Malachi 2:16, God said, *"I hate divorce,"* words giving a clear picture of how he looks at divorce. He didn't stop there, but went on to also condemn physical violence:

"I hate divorce," says the LORD God of Israel, "and I hate a man's covering himself with violence as well as with his garment," says the LORD Almighty. So guard yourself in your spirit, and do not break faith (Malachi 2:16).

"My spouse physically abuses me."
Submitting to physical abuse is not wise. Paul claimed his legal rights when confronted with unlawful physical violence (Acts 25:11). You too have legal rights you can exercise. God established the civil authorities for your protection (Romans 13:1-4).

There were times when King Saul wanted to kill David. Although he was under Saul's authority, David did not stick around when Saul threw a spear at him or plotted to kill him. Instead, he ran away and sought refuge in safe places (1 Samuel 18:11; 19:10-12; 20:42).

If your spouse threatens or commits physical abuse, take whatever steps necessary for your safety. Don't think you are betraying your mate if you seek help. He or she, in fact, is the one who betrayed you by being violent. Do not feel guilty if you take action and do not worry about embarrassing your mate.

Some steps you could take:

- Go to church authorities.

- Call the police.

- Get a temporary restraining order.

- Physically separate with the goal of counseling and rebuilding your marriage—not to divorce. (David physically separated himself from Saul, his king, when Saul wanted to kill him. Yet David continued to honor Saul and desired a restoration of their friendship.)

"I'm to blame for my spouse's violence."

Skeeter and I once witnessed an ugly incident when two close friends, Jerry and Linda, got into an argument in our living room. Linda was much more verbal than Jerry and continuously bombarded him with accusations, complaints, taunts and insults. As she spoke, his frustration grew greater and greater, until he jumped up from his chair, strode across the room, hit her on the shoulder and stomped out of the room.

Should Jerry have hit her? No. Did her words excuse his action? No. Was he responsible for his own behavior? Yes.

But what about Linda? Wasn't she responsible to look at what she had done? Absolutely. Her words had been designed to aggravate Jerry and she succeeded. She needed to prayerfully examine her part, yet not blame herself for his actions.

As you can see, it's reasonable to look at yourself, but don't take this principle too far. Regardless of your part, *never say abuse was okay or justified.* Do not be like Theresa, a woman who told me, "It wasn't his fault he hit me. If I hadn't burned the toast, he wouldn't have been mad."

"I didn't really hurt her."

Men often minimize their actions. Common statements that I have heard include:

- "I didn't hit her with my fist."

- "I just pushed her."

- "I didn't leave any bruises."

- "I only threw her on the bed."

- "I just blocked her from leaving the room."

These defenses do not mean anything to God. He expects husbands to love their wives (Ephesians 5:25) and be gentle (1 Timothy 3:3). Never lay a finger on your wife or block her from leaving the room.

"It's okay for a woman to hit a man."

As I counseled Sherry and Thomas, I learned she had hit and scratched him on many occasions. When I asked her about her violence, she became upset and justified her assaults, saying she only hit him when he ignored her or talked disrespectfully.

Thomas usually responded to the attacks by grabbing her wrists and trying to restrain her. A couple of times when he did this, she said he hurt her wrists and she claimed spousal abuse! In spite of her many attacks, she considered herself the victim. It took several counseling sessions before she was willing to confront her own sin.

Sherry was not unique. I have counseled many women who thought it inexcusable for their husband to be violent, yet who thought it was okay for them as wives to push, hit, slap and throw things at their mate.

 *Personal Application*

Are you or your mate physically abusive?
❏ Yes ❏ No

If you are abusive, write an action plan about how you will stop.

If your spouse is abusive, write an action plan about steps you will take.

Respond to Spiritual Challenges

"My spouse doesn't act like a Christian."

The first six verses of 1 Peter 3 give instructions to wives whose husbands disbelieve or are disobedient to the Bible. In this passage, Peter wrote that the wife should win her husband over *"without words" (verse 1)*, demonstrating a *"gentle and quiet spirit" (verse 4)*. He then went on to say that a husband should treat his wife *"in the same way" (verse 7)*. Strive to win your spouse by your pure and reverent behavior, not by your words.

"My husband wants me to sin."

What should you do if your husband wants you to cheat on your income taxes, watch pornographic movies or lie to your neighbors? The answer is clear: Politely refuse. Read the sobering story of Sapphira, a woman who joined her husband in sin, then suffered death at God's hands (Acts 5:1-10).

 Peter and the other apostles replied: "We must obey God rather than men!" (Acts 5:29).

"My wife wants me to disobey God."

Do not follow your wife's lead if she tries to get you to violate God's Word. Study the example of Adam. He disobeyed God by doing what his wife said, thereby bringing severe consequences upon himself and mankind (Genesis 3:17).

 But Peter and John replied, "Judge for yourselves whether it is right in God's sight to obey you rather than God" (Acts 4:19).

"My spouse doesn't want me to go to church."

You are responsible before God for your actions. Read the Bible and go to church, even if your mate objects. Gently explain that you need these activities and that they help make you a better spouse. However, live a balanced life. Do not engage in so many church activities that you neglect your husband or wife.

"My mate wants me to violate my conscience."

Your spouse may want you to do things that do not violate specific scriptural commands, but which would violate your conscience. Gently refuse, but do not accuse your mate of being immoral. Simply say, "I'm not judging you, but I cannot do that with a good conscience."

 The goal of this command is love, which comes from a pure heart and a good conscience and a sincere faith ... holding on to faith and a good conscience (1 Timothy 1:5, 19).

Although you should not violate your conscience, be aware that you may be bound up with unnecessary rules that have nothing to do with Christianity. If you suspect this might be the case, seek wisdom. Pray about the issues that bother you. Study the Bible. Ask your pastor or a mature Christian of the same sex for advice. Study, yet do not change your behavior unless you are convinced that it is okay with God.

 *Personal Application*

Do you feel pressure from your mate to do something wrong? ❏ Yes ❏ No

If so, what is it?

How will you respond in the future?

Be Wise if Your Wife is Resistant

"My wife is unsubmissive."

If you think your wife has the wrong attitude about submission, look at yourself. Are you are the type of husband described in Chapter 2, focusing on her interests, not yours? When you are a servant-leader, you make it easier for her to trust you and follow your leadership. Ask yourself the following questions:

- Do you make most decisions yourself or as a team?

- Do you talk down to her or treat her with respect?

- Do you criticize her frequently or praise her often?

- Do you order her around or treat her as an equal?

- Do you show anger or patience if she does something wrong?

Once you check your attitude, ask God if you should talk with your wife about hers. Many times the best thing to do is simply pray. Other times it is appropriate to also talk.

If you decide to discuss your concerns, bring them up in a gentle, non-accusatory manner. Show concern for your wife's welfare. Then listen to her response. There may be more to the picture than you realize. Truly seek to understand her point of view.

I still remember one time I had such a discussion with Skeeter. After I finished talking, she gently described many things she had done that week because she wanted to be a good wife. I was humbled.

That's not always the case, of course. You may be right in your observations. If so, after you express your concern, her response is between her and God. It is her responsibility to follow your leadership, not your responsibility to "subject" her. If she disagrees with you, do not become harsh or bitter (Colossians 3:19) or withdraw. Put her in the Lord's hands, keep loving her and walk in the peace of God.

Along similar lines, if you think you need to make a decision when the two of you can't come to a mutual agreement, communicate this clearly and courteously. If she doesn't agree, you could gently say, "Honey, I want to be clear about this. What I said was as the leader of our family. I think this decision is best for the family and hope you will follow it." Once you say this, there usually is no point in getting into an argument. Pray silently that God will give her the grace to follow your leadership. Keep loving her.

✎ *Personal Application*

Do you think your wife resists your leadership?
❑ Yes   ❑ No

If so, write (1) any ways you may have contributed to the problem and (2) what you can do to change.

How will you respond if she ignores your leadership in the future?

Encourage a Passive Husband

"My husband does not lead."

If your husband does not take up his leadership responsibilities, do not try to nag him into doing them. Instead, evaluate yourself to see if his lack of leadership is partly in response to your attitude or behavior. For example, if you have been domineering or have complained a lot about him, he may have given up trying to be a leader. Or he may have gotten lazy because you took over his leadership responsibilities.

Some ways to encourage your husband to take a leadership role are:

- Ask him if you have done anything that makes it difficult for him to lead.

- Ask forgiveness if you have been a poor follower.

- Express respect for him.

- Ask his advice about a problem.

- Don't step in to do things that are his responsibility. Let him do them in his time.

- If he does something differently than you, do not intervene. Let him do it his way.

Although you should usually follow the above guidelines, there may be times when you should assume responsibilities that you wish your husband would take. For example, if he does not participate in family Bible studies with your children, ask him to help out. If he is not willing, do not discontinue the studies. Your children need them.

Pray before taking this sort of action. You may need to take it less often than you think. If you do take steps along these lines, pray not to be resentful or bitter.

✏️ *Personal Application*

Is your husband too passive? ❑ Yes ❑ No

If you checked "yes," review the above suggestions, then write a plan to encourage him as a leader.

"I wish my husband were not so gentle."

Some women do not respect gentleness in a husband. Sensing a power vacuum, they often take on a controlling role.

If you are married to a man who is kind, one who seeks to be a servant-leader, do not see him as "weak." Instead, tell him you appreciate his gentleness and willingly place yourself under his headship.

"I push my husband to be mean."

Sylvia asked me for help because she had been pushing her husband to beat her. From time to time she hit him, and when he didn't strike back, she mocked him, saying, "You're no man."

Why did she do this? She had a history of being abused by men and had come to see physical mistreatment as a sign of love. She thought that when a man hit his wife, it proved he cared for her, since he wanted to control her.

If you act like Sylvia, embark on a serious Bible study of 1 Corinthians 13 and 1 Peter 3:1-6, verses that show what love is. Also seek help from your pastor or his wife to overcome this pattern. You have a lot to unlearn and a lot to learn, yet with God's help you, as did Sylvia, can change.

 *Personal Application*

Do you push your husband to be forceful or mean?
☐ Yes   ☐ No

If you checked "yes," what steps should you take?

Explain Problems to Children

"Our child complains about my mate's behavior."

In Chapter 5, you read that you should support your spouse with your children. But what do you do if your child complains because your mate yells a lot, is an alcoholic or has other serious problems? Your child knows something is wrong and may be scared or confused.

Your first step should be to quietly talk with your spouse in private. Explain how his or her behavior is affecting your child. Be honest, yet also speak with love. Seek a solution.

If this is not successful, it may be appropriate to tell your child, "I love Daddy (or Mommy), but he has an anger problem. Let's pray for him." By talking with your child this way, you acknowledge what's going on, let your child know he or she did not cause the problem, demonstrate love for your spouse and show your child there is something he or she can do: Pray.

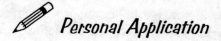 *Personal Application*

Does your child complain about your mate's behavior—or your behavior? ❏ Yes ❏ No

If you checked "yes," how will you deal with this?

Wives, Switch Roles if Necessary

"My husband has severe personal problems."

You are supposed to treat your husband as the leader, yet what do you do if he suffers from Alzheimer's Disease, had a stroke, is an alcoholic or was in an accident resulting in mental incapacity? In such cases, you need to assume more of the leadership role. Do so without guilt, yet still strive to be sensitive to him.

"My husband makes dangerous decisions."

If your husband makes an extremely dangerous decision, or engages in hazardous behavior such as drinking beer while driving, take protective actions. Be wise about how and when you do this, so you don't make things worse. For example, don't grab the steering wheel as he drives. When you act, do so with a loving and respectful attitude.

Read the example of Abigail, a wife who acted contrary to the hasty and foolish decision of Nabal, her husband (1 Samuel 25). His foolish decision nearly resulted in tragedy. In this extreme case, she took care of the situation at night, secretly and independently, then told her husband the next day.

When you are submissive, you act with concern for your husband's best interests. This is sometimes more complex than simply obeying him. On *rare* occasions, your wisest and most loving actions may be contrary to your husband's desires.

Take actions of this sort rarely, if at all. Don't look for excuses to ignore your husband's leadership.

"My husband was a drunkard. Now he's saved."

Perhaps in the past you felt forced to take the leadership role, but things have changed and you feel awkward, wondering if you should redefine your role. This could be the case if your husband was a drunkard but is now sober, was in prison but is now back home, was consumed by work but is now spending more time with the family or was a non-Christian but is now saved and wants to lead family Bible studies.

These changes, although welcome, often create unique problems for a woman who previously was forced to assume the leadership role. In such a case, it usually is not wise to abruptly dump everything in your husband's lap. Instead, talk with him about the issues and gradually redefine your roles.

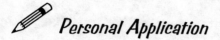 *Personal Application*

Do you need to reverse roles for one of the above reasons? ❑ Yes ❑ No

If so, write your plans for doing so.

A Question for Overcomers

 *Personal Application*

If you experienced any of the problems in this chapter and overcame them, how did you overcome them? What lessons did you learn?

Putting It All Together

Key point: Take action when confronted with serious teamwork problems. Pray for wisdom.

•

Memory verse: *"As iron sharpens iron, so one man sharpens another" (Proverbs 27:17).*

 **Action Plan**

Choose one or two things from this chapter to work on this week.

1.

2.

My Plan

Now that you have finished reading this book, take a few minutes to review each chapter, particularly the "Putting It All Together" section at the end of each chapter. Choose from one to three things to work on in the coming month and write them on this page.

1.

2.

3.

Looking Ahead

The next book in this series, *Putting Money in its Place,* may be the most challenging one for many readers, but it could also be a lifesaver.

Most couples struggle over finances at one time or another. This book will help you deal with many common problems such as:

- ✓ How can we get out of debt?

- ✓ Whose money is it?

- ✓ What about tithing?

- ✓ Is saving different from hoarding?

- ✓ Should we have joint accounts?

- ✓ What if one partner has hidden investments?

- ✓ What guidelines does the Bible give on spending?

- ✓ How can we stop arguing about spending?

- ✓ Is it a sin to want to get rich?

- ✓ Is it biblical to use credit cards?

Join me as we study how to apply God's Word to our bank accounts and credit cards, getting and spending, giving and saving.

More Resources

Author, speaker and marriage and family counselor Doug Britton has helped thousands of people since entering the counseling field in 1967. His ministry focuses on showing how to apply the Word of God to daily life in insightful, practical ways.

Online Daily-Living Bible Studies

Visit www.DougBrittonBooks.com to read and print free online Bible studies on marriage, parenting, depression, jealousy, self-concept, temptation, anger and other daily-living topics.

While at the site, sign up to receive one or two emails each month announcing new online studies, as well as news about new books, seminars and retreats with Doug Britton.

Seminars and Retreats

Doug teaches on a wide variety of topics at seminars and retreats. Subject matter includes marriage, parenting, biblical counseling, depression, jealousy and insecurity, self-concept, finances, temptation and anger. For information about sponsoring a seminar or retreat at your church or community center, go to www.DougBrittonBooks.com.

See next page for more resources

Practical Books for Daily Living

Learn how to apply the Bible's truths in all areas of your life. If the following books by Doug Britton are not available at your local bookstore, you can purchase them online at www.DougBrittonBooks.com.

- **Conquering Depression:** A Journey Out of Darkness into God's Light
- **Defeating Temptation:** Biblical Secrets to Self-Control
- **Getting Started:** Taking New Steps in My Walk with Jesus
- **Healing Life's Hurts:** God's Solutions When Others Wound You
- **Overcoming Jealousy and Insecurity:** Biblical Steps to Living without Fear
- **Self-Concept:** Understanding Who You are in Christ
- **Strengthening Your Marriage:** 12 Exercises for Married Couples
- **Successful Christian Parenting:** Nurturing with Insight and Disciplining in Love
- **Victory over Grumpiness, Irritation and Anger**

Marriage by the Book (eight-book series)
- **Book 1 – Laying a Solid Foundation**
- **Book 2 – Making Christ the Cornerstone**
- **Book 3 – Encouraging Your Spouse**
- **Book 4 – Extending Grace to Your Mate**
- **Book 5 – Talking with Respect and Love**
- **Book 6 – Improving Your Teamwork**
- **Book 7 – Putting Money in its Place**
- **Book 8 – Fanning the Flames of Romance**
- **Marriage by the Book Group Leaders' Guide**